Marcel Péroche was born in 1907 and by the age of 14 he had gained a place in the State's railway workshops, determined to rise to the position of an elite driver of the majestic Pacific Class locomotives.

This he did, but not before thirty years rising through the ranks. He guides us through these years on the footplate, not forgetting to give the turbulent social background of the 1920s and 30s.

When war breaks out he is sent to Syria to work the Orient Express and we experience the thirst, the blistering heat and the difficulties of the task. He returns to his beloved France and the German occupation. But Péroche is far too wise and human to tar all the occupiers with the same brush. He speaks of his German railway counterparts with respect and sometimes even admiration. In a moving passage he speaks of a German depot manager's offer to celebrate the coming Liberation and he reflects on the folly of war.

With the arrival of the Americans in 1944 Péroche has new bosses and as the Germans retreat, the whole of France turns to reconstruction. Péroche paints a graphic picture of the difficulty of running a railway with tunnels blocked and bridges down.

The story concludes with the end of the steam era and Péroche's regrets. His life was hard and, at times, dangerous, 'but the rewards were sweet. The driver on the footplate of a Pacific was like the captain of a ship on the bridge: the sole master aboard after God.'

Pacific Senator
A Train Driver's Life

Marcel Péroche

translation and introduction
Roland Wilson

Argyll
publishing

© translation Roland Wilson

First published Berger-Levrault 1984
First published in this translation 2005
Argyll Publishing
Glendaruel
Argyll PA22 3AE
Scotland
www.argyllpublishing.com

British Library Cataloguing-in-Publication Data.
A catalogue record for this book is available from
the British Library.

ISBN 1 902831 85 3

Origination: Cordfall Ltd, Glasgow

Printing: Bell & Bain Ltd, Glasgow

Contents

Translator's note

The majority of railway terms have direct English translations but I have kept the names of the main railway agents in French. This is because they are fairly simple to follow and give the text a French feel. By far the most common is the term *chef* with the following noun usually similar to the English or a common French word. e.g. *chef de gare* is station master, *chef de depôt* is depot manager etc.

Some, however, require a little more explanation. The *chef de feuille* was the person responsible for allocating loco and rolling stock to form a train and then designate a train crew to man it. The *feuille* was the sheet of paper with the orders written on it.

The *chef mécanicien* was the head driver in the depot. He was a manager responsible not only for overseeing the drivers daily, but also for testing those taking tests or examinations.

I have also retained the French words for the three main departments in the French railways: *traction, exploitation* and *voie*. The first, and most important, was *traction*, which looked after locos and rolling stock, *exploitation* was in charge of the stations and *voie* was the department monitoring signals and the track.

Foreword

THERE ARE few people who read a book as closely and as critically as a translator. The task of translating Marcel Péroche's memoirs presented two problems. The first was to somehow convey the man Péroche. His style of writing seems unpretentious and accessible and we discover his underlying patriotism, his pacificism but most of all his transparent love of his fellow man. When he encounters men who seem to have no redeeming virtues Péroche will find one nevertheless.

During the occupation he has unashamed respect and even affection for the German railwaymen sent to run his beloved country's railway. For him, the ties that bind working men and women are infinitely stronger than the crude enmity nurtured by arrogant and cruel business and national interests. His images and analogies are those of the common people, he has no time for literary or classical allusion.

As a 'chauffeur', a fireman, then a 'mécanicien' or engine driver he was already in a respected, well-paid layer of the working class. But as the driver of a Pacific locomotive, a prestigious, handsome and powerful affair, he was a member of the railway elite and so entitled to the rank of 'senator'. Consequently his language is hardly ever vulgar except when unavoidable. When speaking of a class of engine known as the Willotos (a modified Pacific) he says: 'On les appelait les 'putains' parce qu'elles n'avaient pas de mécaniciens titulaires.' This means that they were called whores because they didn't have the same driver for every journey!

Péroche is most comfortable when describing his relationship with the steam locomotives and at times we feel that his narrative on the other things in life are slightly forced.

Nevertheless, all that he tells is tied into the main thread of his story which is about how sensible, rewarding, but at times dangerous, are the simple, human things in life.

The political backdrop

Inevitably he alludes to movements in French history that are less well known to English speaking readers. In the first chapter he mentions the massive strikes of 1920. These were provoked by the government of the *'Bloc National'*, elected in November 1919. This was a right wing coalition, which had been voted to power as a reaction against the anarchic period after the war. It is simplistic to claim that the French workers' unrest after the war was guided by Moscow. The government had courted France's main trade union, the *Confédération Générale du Travail (CGT)* during the war in order to maximise nationalised industrial output. By 1919 the private sector were naturally claiming similar treatment. The economy was in tatters, inflation rife and in May 1919 strikes broke out.

Clemenceau, who had remained caretaker prime minister on the signing of the armistice, decided that industrial peace could be bought by concessions. On 23 April 1919 the 8 hour working day was voted by the French parliament. The application of the law was confused. Clemenceau proposed little by little and sector by sector. The workers proposed a blanket application immediately. What was planned as a palliative had merely aggravated the unrest.

It was now that part of the frustrated French working class began to look more sympathetically at the Russian example. By mid-1919 there was open dissension between the CGT and those who turned to Russia for a lead.

For its part, the French government participated in the allied intervention against Russia but only in a support role. This was seen by the French as the nation being dragged into yet another long war. A decision to withdraw was forced when André Marty led the mutiny of the French Black Sea fleet, sent to harass the Russian revolutionaries. It is against this post war background of social unrest fuelled by high prices and external revolutionary influence that the reactionary government of the *'Bloc National'* was elected. On 18 January 1920 Clemenceau resigned as prime minister and was replaced by the right wing

Alexandre Millerand. His agenda was short and simple: reparations from Germany to enrich France and the suppression of the revolutionary movement to ensure industrial peace. When Péroche mentions the strikes of May 1920 these were the final throes of a wave which started in February. The reasons for the unrest were first, the ongoing inflation and economic hardship and second, the desperate bid by the communists for recognition. As mentioned above the left did badly in the 1919 elections. Consequently, the revolutionary 'nothing to lose' tendency pushed to the fore.

The strikes, as Péroche writes, provoked a harsh reaction by the newly installed reactionary government. Blackleg workers and managers amongst others were recruited to run the railways. Some 15,000 railwaymen lost their jobs. The strike leader, Gaston Monmousseau, was imprisoned and legal action was taken out against the CGT. The defeat was humiliating. On 21 May 1920 the CGT ordered all its members back to work. Worst of all was the aftermath. The CGT was legally dissolved, albeit with a suspended sentence on appeal. Members left in droves. Finally it was discovered that only 20% of CGT members had supported the strikes anyway. The French trade union movement had been blown apart.

The SNCF

As with all railways, the French began development by simple concessions. This was fairly arbitrary until 1842 with some concessions in perpetuity and others for 99 years. The first attempt at rationalisation was the 1842 charter. This stated that the government bought the land, mapped the line and paid for the infrastructure. It was then leased to the companies for 99 years, after which it would revert to the state. In 1850 there were 28 railway companies, 19 in 1852 and 14 in 1857. This trend towards concentration accelerated in 1852 when the government declared that there should only be six companies: The Northern Region, Paris-Orleans line (PO), the Midi Region, the Western Region, the Eastern Region and the Paris-Lyon-Mediterranean (PLM) line. Of these six, the Northern was by far the most prestigious and profitable with its maritime links.

The next major step towards nationalisation was in 1878 with the Freycinet plan. The object of the exercise was to encourage railway companies to service loss making lines by massive government subsidies. In return for the government renouncing rights to forced buyouts, the companies undertook to link smaller towns and keep ticket prices down. By 1900 some three-quarters of rail passengers had access to reduced fares. Seven years later in 1907 the state made its first direct move towards nationalisation and bought the Western Region which was on the verge of bankruptcy. The investment became a bottomless financial hole for the government.

But it was the First World War that gave the French state its first opportunity to run the railways. Unsurprisingly, in January 1914, the entire network was put under the control of the Ministry for War and the railway companies found themselves under one authority with no redress whatsoever. The Northern Region was virtually overrun by the war along with a quarter of the Eastern Region.

By 1918 the railways were in a terrible condition, lacking rolling stock and locomotives. Moreover the network itself has been under-maintained for four years. Consequently, the government intervened with the creation of *un fond commun* or a development fund of sorts, along with an umbrella *Conseil Directeur des Chemins de Fer* to give a coherent national plan. In short the idea was that the fund would cover the difference between income from fares and freight charges and expenditure on wages, maintenance and development. Fares were to be increased gradually so that the fund would become redundant – hopefully by 1927. This proved to be wishful thinking. By 1933 the deficit stood at 3.85bn francs.

The crisis of the 30s, the hardship endured by the population following reductions in wages and the growing threat of fascism forged a new political alliance: *Le Front Populaire*. The *Front* came to power in May 1936. Léon Blum was at the helm but in fact the government was drifting rudderless. Social unrest continued and the rise of Hitler's Nazi party made the *Front*'s pacifism and disarmament policies look dangerous. Like Clemenceau before him in 1919, Blum carried through important social reforms in an effort to defuse the situation: paid holidays, the forty hour week and the nationalisation of the *Banque de France*. But on 8th of May 1938 his cabinet fell. It was in this atmosphere of social confusion, financial difficulties and the growing German threat that calls for some sort of re-organisation of the railways grew. Some said that the railways benefited private interests and neglected their collective role. Some claimed that the railway directors were in fact *dictateurs du rail*. Some economists argued that the railway's need for virtually unlimited finance needed a new form of corporate structure.

The grim situation played into the hands of the CGT, which had continually pressed for nationalisation as the only solution. Yet the government and many others were not convinced of the wisdom of total nationalisation and so the idea of semi-nationalisation was born. After many inter-ministry commissions and endless negotiations with the rail companies an agreement was concluded.

The *Société Nationale des Chemins de Fer* or *SNCF* was founded on 1 January 1938. It would have the right to operate the French railways for 45 years, until 1982 (the French government took total control in 1983). The government held 51% and the railway companies 49%. From that day on the SNCF would be funded by the Treasury.

The Occupation, the Resistance and the Liberation
Péroche's first hand accounts of life during the occupation, his links with the Railway Resistance (*Résistance Fer*) and the liberation in 1944 are valuable. However, he does not often give generalisations. This avoidance of giving background information is possibly due to the controversies, that continue to this day, on the role of the SNCF during the occupation, the value of the work of the Resistance and the conduct of the Americans when they took over the railways in June 1944.

The principal criticism of the SNCF during the war was its collaboration with the Germans on the deportation of the Jews. It would be difficult to blame individual railwaymen since they were governed by Article 155 of the legal military code which inflicted the death penalty or deportation for refusing to obey orders. What is clear, however, is that the SNCF did not protest against having to carry out this gruesome task. In a bizarre, historical move the SNCF continued to press for payment for these services just after the liberation. [1] Needless to say the SNCF is still reluctant to give historians access to the archives for the period 1938-48.

As for the French Resistance, Péroche's remarks, sometimes caustic, give a fair reflection of the situation overall. There can be no doubt that the SNCF's chief use for the Allies was information. Railway staff had prior knowledge of all troop and logistics movements and this was duly passed on to London. On the issue of sabotage the relationship was less stable. However there were hundreds of branch lines and re-routing trains when a main line was severed was a simple task. Bridges and viaducts were the key targets and these were well guarded by the Germans. The second issue was that of sabotaging locomotives. In his book on the 1944 allied bombing raids over France Y. Machefert-Tassin shows that German military needs were met throughout the period and that it was France's domestic rail transport that suffered. In short, the *Wehrmacht* had first call on locomotives and rolling stock and as a rule, engine sabotage merely made life more difficult for the French. [2]

Given its clandestine nature, the French Resistance was not a national organisation. Specific tasks were given to certain local resistance groups but when a national offensive was called for, such as on 6 June 1944, the Resistance could not be relied on. In a trial run in 1943, for example, the Resistance in the Midi was given 50 objectives. Only 15 were eliminated and, moreover, local groups did not hesitate to change these objectives if they saw fit. [3] It was partly this weak link that encouraged Eisenhower to press ahead with his plan for carpet bombing and the ensuing destruction that Péroche witnessed at Cherbourg and Caen.

Finally, a few words are called for on Péroche's account of the relationship between the American railwaymen and the French from June 1944 onwards. The Americans had been storing vast numbers of railway locomotives and rolling stock

---

(1) *Le Rail au Service de la Liberté*: B. Carriere, La Vie du Rail 2004. p.7

(2) *Une Saison en Enfer*: G. Ribeill & Y. Machefert-Tassin, published privately 2004. p. 204

(3) *Le Rail au Service de la Liberté*: Bruno Carriere, La Vie du Rail 2004. p. 13

in Britain since 1942. All trains were headed by two locomotives, hence, the somewhat cavalier American approach to abandoning broken engines.

Péroche certainly mentions the problem of language but does not speak of the undercurrent of Franco-American mistrust. This was due to the Americans' highly authoritarian policy. There was little or no communication or collaboration at the time. For example, the Americans initially ran all trains on the right – the opposite of French regulations. This meant that all signalling equipment became redundant and clearly increased the risk of accidents. Needless to say the Americans soon realised the folly of such a decision and reverted to orthodox French running. [4]

But what the French admired was American fearlessness. An apprentice driver, Georges Soulié, gives an example.

'This was something I witnessed a few times. We're steaming along and suddenly an axle box on one of the wagons overheats and starts to smoke. It's a munitions train. The driver in charge (always an American) stops the train in the middle of nowhere, but preferably on an embankment. We uncouple the damaged wagon and get as many jacks as we can lay our hands on. The wagon, full of shells rolls down the embankment. We couple up the rest of the train and carry on. It was war and there was no wasting time.'

On another occasion the American engineer in charge tells him to place the air-brake valve in the wrong position. He argues. The American pulls out his pistol. That's the valve position on engines in the States but not on a British 2-8-0. The train, loaded with munitions, moves off with no air pressure. Soulié finally persuades the American that he's in the wrong, but has to risk his life for it. He concludes, however:

'It wasn't a question of whether I was happy working in these bizarre conditions or not. One thing is certain. I'll never forget that the men from 'over there' were in France to free us – and for that we have to thank them.' [5]

---

(4) *Le Rail au Service de la Liberté* p.51

(5) *Ibid* p.53

The technical aspect

Second was the challenge of the technical details of the job. For this I had the good fortune to have Semmens and Goldfinch's book *How Steam Locomotives Really Work*. [6] The general reader may become frustrated with Péroche's obsession with an item known as fusible plugs and a short word of explanation is perhaps called for. A steam engine crew stood behind a metal box, known as the boiler, which was in fact a potential bomb. Recognising this, the designers went to some lengths to ensure that the device would never explode. Inevitably they factored in a margin of safety – when a fuel gauge in a car reads empty, the driver assumes there is always a bit left. Drivers knew about safety margins, they knew that boilers were tested to double the permitted pressure for example. One thing, however, was difficult to convey to the crew and that was just how much water there was in the boiler. There was a glass gauge fixed in the cab which gave the water level inside the boiler. When the locomotive was static on level track the gauge gave one reading. But clearly when the engine was on even a slight gradient or descent the reading was corrupted (see diagram p.141). Dedicated drivers who manned the same locomotive every day perhaps got overconfident about knowing what this variable actually was. Did this mean then, that when there was no water 'in the glass' that there was no water in the boiler? Not at all. It meant that there was a little water above the top of the boiler (known as the crown plate) and that water should be introduced, or 'injected', into the boiler immediately.

And if there was no water in the tender to inject? Then there was another method of measurement, using water valves next to the glass to see not how much, but just how little water was left above the crown plate. If the lowest valve was opened and only steam came out, then that meant there was no water above the plate worth speaking of.

So much for the preliminaries.

When the water on the top of the boiler ran dry the last safety device was activated: the fusible plugs. These were two

---

(6) *How Steam Locomotives Really Work* P. Semmens & A. Goldfinch, Oxford 2000

copper plugs placed between the bottom of the boiler and the top of the firebox. The seal was made of an alloy with a melting point below that of the copper plug itself. The seal melted when the heat was more than that of the water in the boiler, which was normally regularly replenished by cold water through the injectors. When there was no water, however, they melted and allowed the remaining pressurised steam to pass through the plug hole into the firebox. This would not necessarily put out the fire, but the noise of the plugs being ejected by the steam with a bang and the noise of escaping steam were meant to alert the crews that all was not well and the engine should be stopped then the fire 'dropped' onto the track. This was an embarrassing event since it reflected a crew that had misjudged the amount of water needed for the run or who had used what water they had, carelessly. For Péroche it was the driver's nightmare since it was always followed by a enquiry, a severe reprimand and a dented bonus.

Failure to stop the engine and drop the fire inevitably led to an explosion and the crew would then likely travel the first leg of their final journey to the great engine depot in the sky.

As for the other railway details, Péroche crafts into the narrative explanations of what the various controls were for and what the essentials of professional engine driving consisted of. What is certain is that when diesel and electric locomotives were introduced the skills of the driver and fireman became redundant. Péroche's book helps to keep the memory of these skills both accessible and alive.

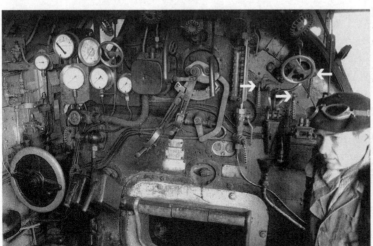

Photo showing the three valves which indicated how little water was left above the crown plate. If the lowest valve was opened and only steam came out, then that meant there was no water above the plate worth speaking of.

Pacific Senator
A Train Driver's Life

Marcel Péroche

Inside the cab of a Pacific (Collection Violet)

Péroche (on the right) with his fireman when serving in Syria

A Dog's Life

I'VE SPENT the best part of my life on the railways and I wouldn't have had it any other way – not for anything in the world. Right from being a boy I dreamed of that wandering life where you spend more time on your engine than with your wife and children. When I was twelve I used to stand on the Diconche bridge over the river Charente and all afternoon I'd watch the Paris-Royan trains run under. The fast trains sped by at over 100 kilometres an hour, but you could still make out the driver, with his big goggles, leaning out of the cab to see the signals up ahead more clearly and glimpse the fireman hard at work.

In the following years, experience taught me that crewing steam locos was a dog's life but I loved it. If I had to live this life again I'd follow exactly the same profession. In those days there was no question of special working conditions and you had to be tough skinned to survive. In winter we were outside all the time and the fireman was always soaking with sweat and freezing rain. When it was foggy, the driver had to peer at the track ahead for hours on end to check the signals.

Summer, in fact, was sometimes worse. It was thirst, especially on shunting duty when you were working in the marshalling yards under the blazing sun at 50^0 on the footplate and choking coal dust. The water in the stations was usually ice cold and we drank litres of it, more often than not from a bucket. Yet crewmen were rarely ill. I've never missed a day's work on account of illness.

Nights too were hard. When I was working Pacifics on the Paris-Thouars link I was on the footplate four nights running without really getting a good sleep during the day. On each run the fireman handled 5 or 6 tons of coal and when he wasn't shovelling he was raking and looking after the firebed. But we found all that normal.

So why choose such a profession? First, because we were well paid and we retired at fifty. But that was not the most important thing. Above all it was an active, adventurous life. And when you got a driver and fireman who understood each other perfectly it gave a feeling of being a real team.

In those days energy wasn't simply on tap and you had to have the knowhow to produce the steam efficiently to haul the trains. The fireman had to have a talent for building his fire and he had to accept the struggle of coping with his ever-hungry beast. As for the driver, he had to use the steam his partner produced as wisely as possible and adapted continually to the profile of the road ahead. But the train crews had to avoid committing the most serious fault of all – and the most severely punished – the melting of the lead safety plugs which could, in some cases, lead to the boiler exploding.

You had to like responsibility too. There was no room for error in a driver's life. If signalling or braking rules were transgressed, catastrophe could follow. But the rewards were sweet. The driver on the footplate was like the captain on the bridge: the sole master aboard after God.

CHAPTER 1
Apprentice

I WAS seven when the First World War broke out. My father worked in a bakery and despite long days, lasting sometimes fourteen or fifteen hours, he earned very little. My mother was continually ill because one of her kidneys had been dislocated at my birth. She had an operation but the surgeons at the time didn't manage to graft the kidneys back into place, doubtless because they lacked the skills of today.

Since father had four children, not to mention housing my grandmother, he hoped to escape being sent to the front. Also, he had never done military service. His hopes were dashed when he was called up in October 1914. He left Saintes to carry out his training as an infantryman in the Songes camp near Bordeaux. France's problems meant that family interests took second place. In early November he was posted to the Vosges and was wounded the following year.

Although my mother was an ironing lady she couldn't work on account of her ill health and so we had to make do with the family allowance. I can say that my brothers, sister and myself had an unhappy childhood – extremely unhappy in fact. Hunger often brought us to tears, but there was nothing unusual in this. Many families suffered the same. In a bid to escape a diet of dry bread we would hunt for mushrooms, collect chestnuts in the woods and gather windfalls from the orchards. We even managed to make wine with plums using brown sugar, which was cheaper than refined. Just after the grape harvest was the time to strip the vines of the few grapes left. With our brown sugar we almost managed to make a palatable beverage. Towards the end of the war the Americans disembarked at Bordeaux and Verdon with masses of equipment and food supplies.

Those coming through Bordeaux took the train as far as Pons. From there the officers used to march them to Saintes on a so-called training exercise. We would set off at daybreak, tramping forty kilometres there and back, barefoot, so as to save the shoe leather for Sunday mass. On the way back, we'd bring them water, blackberries and sometimes grapes. Realising our pitiful state, they gave us tins of corned beef and fruit as a reward. When we got home my mother and grandmother were wide-eyed in amazement. My mother was always a bit worried since hunger came before honesty in those days. 'You didn't steal it?' she'd ask. 'No, it was the Americans.' Then grandma would raise her eyes to the Heavens and say, 'God Bless the Americans.'

At last, the war ended on 11 November 1918. Our parents insisted that we all get our National Education Certificate so as to get a reasonable job. 1919 was my final year at school, but I was a very poor performer, since I hadn't learnt much in the previous years. During the war anything went and we were too busy looking for food to take school seriously. Luckily for me, a new headmaster (from Fort sur Bironde) was appointed. He promised my parents that I'd get my certificate but only as long as he had a free hand in the affair. More often than not, his hands were free indeed! I have sharp memories of this, but have to thank him for using Draconian methods, because it was thanks to them that I succeeded reasonably well.

It was just after getting my school certificate in June 1920 at the age of thirteen that I turned my attention to learning a trade. At that time, Saintes was a major railhead, more so than today. There were railway workshops, a vast loco depot and a maintenance workshop for rolling stock.

There were three major divisions looking after the railways. The first, and most important, was *traction*, which involved locos and rolling stock, *exploitation*, was in charge of the stations and *voie* was the department monitoring signals and the track.

Saintes, being in the Western Region, was within the state-controlled section of the railways. At that time it covered

Normandy, Brittany and West France. The other regions, such as the East France and the Paris-Lyon-Mediterranean line (PLM) were in private hands. For a long time, however, the railwaymen had wanted the entire network to be nationalised. In May 1920 the biggest strike in the history of the railways broke out. [1] Over the previous months the powerful CGT had not only gained several concessions on the employment front but was also advocating total nationalisation. At Saintes, almost all those in the workshops toed the union line, but in *traction*, *exploitation* and *voie* only the hardliners went on strike. [2]

We used our Thursday rest days to go to the meetings organised by the strikers. These were at Acacias on the road to Lormont or at Maine. The main leaders would mount the podium and rally the strikers: 'Hang on in there comrades and we'll get what's rightly ours!'

When the speeches were over the strikers would form a procession of some seven or eight hundred men with placards and banners. Led by the band, they crossed the town in full song. When they reached the Senator's house, the procession stopped. The band struck up the International and soon everybody was singing. Suddenly the shutters of this well-appointed abode would be closed because those inside were terrified of the 'Reds' as they were called.

So as to be fair, the procession then went to the town hall where the mayor was treated to the same serenade. Around midday the gathering broke up and folk went home.

After going through the same scenario for a fortnight, the strikers began to show a certain lassitude. There was now no money coming into the house and things started to turn nasty. But there was no question of giving in. The line had to be held at all cost. The worst off sold their furniture, linen and I even heard of gold wedding rings being pawned. In the meetings

(1) The wave of strikes in Spring 1920 were a desperate reaction by the left to the overwhelming victory of the right in the 1919 elections.

(2) Péroche makes the distinction between those employed in the workshops and those employed in actually running the trains. Overall, only 20% of members obeyed the CGT (Confédération Générale du Travail) union strike call.

and processions the singing lost its heartiness and a certain sadness crept in.

Of course, this was just what the managers had been waiting for to incite the strikers to get back to work. They tried to get them into a corner by announcing deadlines. If, on such and such a day the men were back at work, they promised that there would be no questions asked and no reprisals. But in those days there was no radio or television and I've never been able to find out if the details of these deals were ever passed on to the rank and file.

Finally the management gave an ultimatum. All those not respecting the deadline for returning to work would lose their jobs. The men probably didn't believe these threats and carried on demonstrating. But then, on the last day, with their tails between their legs, most were back at work.

In 1920 the majority of deputies were right wing and the government was known as the *Chambre Bleu Horizon*.[3] Pierre Tattinger was the Saintes' deputy and he was set on making an example of those who had refused to go back to work by the deadline. This example consisted of shutting down the Saintes workshops and the 2,000 men who had held out to the bitter end found themselves on the street.

On the other hand, those who had refused to strike were pampered by the management. One of these, who also ran the rugby team, suffered humiliation at the hands of the strikers. One evening they waited for him after work, jumped and stripped him then painted him yellow. I can still remember seeing him careering through the streets clad only in his underpants.

The workshops didn't stay closed long. During the summer, the State rented them to a private company called the CIMT,[4] which in turn, handed over the running of the affair to Carde, which was a Bordeaux concern. The sacked workers were taken back, but on private industry terms. That meant

(3) So called because of the majority of First World War veterans in the Chamber of Deputies who wore their blue uniforms to the assemblies.

(4) *Compagnie Industrielle de Matériel de Transport*. A privately owned engineering company.

they lost a fortnight's holidays, pension rights, free travel and other benefits. But the most important thing for me was the training college which looked after the young apprentices in the State section of the railways. The CIMT didn't want to finance it since it had a lease for only fifteen years. Fortunately, the State took over the school and set the opening date at 1 October 1920.

Consequently, in September I applied to learn a trade and, of course, eventually to become a qualified railwayman. For this you had to have the school certificate and pass the entrance exam. I had the former and applied to take the latter. There were only fifty places for two hundred applicants but I had the good fortune to come sixteenth – quite a creditable performance.

I started, therefore, on 1 October. The day was divided into five hours in the workshops and three for theory, which covered technology, drawing, French and computation. We even had lessons on something which has now disappeared: ethics! In the first year we were paid 6 francs a month, in the second, 10 francs and the third, 12 francs. In order to give us the choice of a profession we spent a fortnight in each of the main trades used in the railways.

First we learnt filing, turning and assembly before going on to joinery, forged metalwork, boiler making and lastly upholstery. Once we had done the round of the different workshops we made our choice after taking into account the instructor's comments. My instructor thought I had the aptitude for forged metalworking but I preferred assembly. I was perhaps less gifted for this trade but despite this, I succeeded. Today I'm certain I made the right choice because for an engine driver a training in assembly is a lot more useful than that of a forged metal worker. After having worked ten years on steam locos, I know them inside out and consequently I can get any train to its destination even if it means some running repairs.

It was at training college that I was introduced to the game of rugby. The head, Monsieur Longeville was from Perigueux and had been in the Navy. He insisted the students took sports and had a real weakness for a rugby ball. With money hard to come by, he made do with what he could lay his hands on. He asked the head upholsterer in the workshops to craft a ball using moleskin. The result was not exactly a rugby ball – but it was oval and better than nothing.

Until then I had never played rugby nor took an interest in athletics, since football was the only game we played. I was ragged by the others when they heard this: 'Football's for girls!' they jeered or 'for folk with no hands! Frightened of getting hurt are we?'

Consequently I trained to pass, catch and gather the ball and learned the basic rules of the game.

Right from the first matches it was decided that I should be in the backs and since I could run well I played on the wing. The pitch was the college recreation ground, which was covered in ash from the locos and had not a single blade of grass on it. It's pointless to describe the state we were in at the end of the game. We didn't show mercy when we tackled despite the surface of the pitch; consequently the skin on our knees and elbows didn't stay long and on seeing us covered in blood, Monsieur Longeville would say: 'Bah! That's nothing; it's the only way to learn the game. It'll heal, you'll see.'

His passion for the game was so contagious that soon rugby took up all my spare time. I moved up the ranks. Soon I was the winger in the Saintes Rugby Club's first team. The Saintes team played in the First Division championship and so I met some of the elite of French rugby when I was quite young. Many became friends with some becoming famous in entertainment and politics. I'm as keen today on rugby as I was sixty years ago.

After three years at college I passed the junior apprenticeship exams and was given a place in the workshops as a senior apprentice, first in assembly and then with the team working on connecting and driving rods.

All my spare time went on sports and when the rugby season was over it was athletics during the summer months. I trained for the 100 and 200 metres and the 4 x 100 metres relay. It was in the training sessions and competitions I made friends with a typesetter who was a bit older than me and who had three sisters. In late August 1925 after coming home from an athletics meeting I went to the Parc Marine to an open air party at Saint-Vivien. I'd only just arrived when this good-looking young brunette came up.

'Are you Marcel Péroche?' she said.

'That's me.'

'My brother's often talked about you. You do athletics with him and play rugby, don't you?'

'That's right.'

'I'm his sister, Antoinette. How about joining me for the Lancers' Foursome?'

'I'm afraid that's out of the question. Dancing terrifies me!'

She seemed surprised. In fact at that time I never went to dance halls, first, because I gave all my wages to grandma and she wasn't exactly a generous woman. And second, our trainer had told us all to get a good night's sleep before matches. That meant no late nights on Saturdays and no dancing.

However, the beautiful Antoinette didn't rejoin her friends for the Lancers' Foursome.

'Don't let me stop you,' I said.

'Do you know,' she went on, 'I'm not a great fan of dancing myself.'

And we remained together for the rest of the evening.

She too was in financial straits. Her father had died two or three years before, which meant her mother had to work to supplement the wages her brother got from the print shop. Antoinette was a young seamstress at the Bouyer sisters' shop since they had kept her on after her apprenticeship.

The town of Saintes at that time was served by a narrow gauge train, pulled by a steam engine and every morning on my way to the workshops I'd wave to Antoinette from the carriage I was in. She'd give me a wave back, but making sure none of the three sisters saw her since had they known, it would have been a real to do.

At first she was just a good friend, but as the weeks went by we saw each other more often.

When the rugby season started I had to wangle a bit of money from grandma so that I could pay my subs. The team president at the time was a well-known surgeon who had given all the team members a white, blue-lined woolen sweater which must have cost a small fortune.

'The team won't catch a chill before the kick off now!' he joked.

So just before kick-off we used to go onto the pitch, flicking the ball about in front of the tribune all decked out in our fine white sweaters. The local girls would make a fuss about keeping their man's sweater on their knees during the match. Obviously I entrusted mine to Antoinette.

We'd meet up at the exit after the match and pooling our money would sometimes have enough for the pictures.

That lasted until May 1927, when I left for military service in the Third Constantine Artillery Division in Algeria. I was posted as blacksmith and for a year and a half I lived an uneventful existence. Antoinette would write twice a week and sent a parcel every month. Only sports broke the boredom. There was athletics in the form of the 200 metres and rugby. On several occasions we had matches against Bone, Algiers and Bizerte and there was even a match against the British Royal Navy. The Navy team was captained by the scrum-half who played for England.

Things had changed when I got back at the workshops in October 1928. The *Aciers du Nord* had taken over from the Carde company – but still under the CIMT. The new management was more aggressive and made up of young graduates fresh out of the *Centrale, Arts et Metiers* and other *Grandes Ecoles*. [5] They were ambitious and talented, but above all, they were ready to sacrifice quality for profit. First on their agenda was the payroll. Consequently, the team looking after

(5) Grandes Ecoles are the state's own professional establishments. Those graduating from the Grandes Ecoles initially served the State but with the growth of private industry they were soon to be found outside nationalised industries.

A Mikado in the
workshop for
an overhaul
(Collection
Viollet)

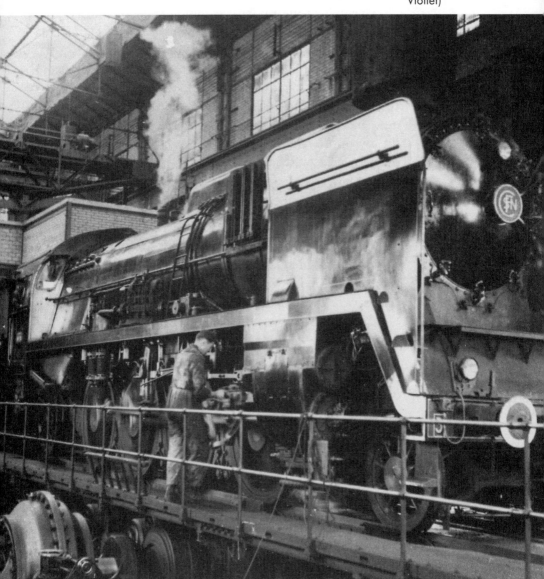

the driving wheel gear, seven or eight of us when I'd left, was now down to four. A fair number of railwaymen had been laid off, especially single men, and job changes were the order of the day.

The least you could say was that it wasn't the best time to be back at my old job.

'Monsieur Péroche,' I was told politely, 'We are in the middle of reorganising the company. It's impossible to take you on again just now.'

Unemployment was fairly common at the time and I wasn't over keen to move to Michelin at Clermont Ferrand. One of my brothers worked there and I'd spent a few day in 'Tyre City' [6] as it used to be called. The Clermont rugby team had made me an offer to play wing in the team, which meant I could have got into Michelin quite easily. But the Saintes managers wanted to keep me. The president at that time was the owner of a wood-products factory at Bellevue and he took me on while I waited for better times.

For a month or so I worked on a machine making spokes for wheelbarrows and car wheels. I was under a foreman who had no time for joking because his only interest was getting the job done. I used to amuse myself watching him when the rugby club president came. He'd always search me out and we'd talk rugby. He was so obsessed with the game that on Mondays he'd spend an hour with me, or more, going over Sunday's game. I'd see my foreman frown since he was obviously more interested in the work than in rugby. He'd wait for the president to go and then he'd needle me. I took real pleasure in telling him, 'Why don't you tell the boss? He's the one that put me here.'

One day in early November, a friend of mine from the old workshop team called on my parents. He was a fresh-faced fellow from Perigord who was a team supervisor. He told them that he wanted to see me urgently to present me to the CIMT with a view to getting a job in the team again. When I got back from the wood factory I rushed to see him. At last I'd get into the railways.

---

(6) So called because of the predominance of the Michelin company in Clermont Ferrand.

However, it wasn't all good news because management was asking a high return with demanding shifts. The job included a 4 o'clock to midnight shift on Sundays so that the connecting-rod sections would be ready for mounting on the Monday morning. My problem was that it meant missing the Sunday afternoon match. Since I had little choice I was forced to accept.

In the end I managed to get the best of both worlds. When we had an away game I found a replacement at the workshops. When it was a home game I booked in at four in the morning after a three kilometre walk and booked out at midday. When I got home I'd have a light meal and a coffee strong enough to raise the dead. Then all I had to do was to get changed ready for the match. After all that I could still run! These days the players are well rested and get to the venue by car. They might even have someone to play the match for them for all I know!

During the winter I split my time between bearings and rugby balls. But in Spring 1929 Saintes was hit by a bombshell.

The State's rail network, which was the biggest in France, was nevertheless wide open to criticism in those days. The government at the time realised that it was essential to get its house in order and, moreover, the problems thrown up by the 1920s' strikes and the demands of the railwaymen had still not been resolved. In order to get this massive problem sorted out, the government needed a man who had the authority to make decisions but at the same time understand the human problems that lay behind them. Men like this didn't come ten a penny, yet the government found the man of the moment.

Raoul Dautry was from a polytechnic [7] and former manager in the Northern Region. He was appointed Director in 1929 and destined to become the War Minister in the Second War then Minister for the Reconstruction and Urban Development at the Liberation. He died in 1951, but all railwaymen, especially those lower down the hierarchy, remember him always. During the years he was at the head of the State railways a good few stories were told about him.

---

(7) These have a similar status to the Grandes Ecoles with the emphasis on intellectual ability rather than practical experience.

Everything he said and did spread over the network like wildfire. I honestly think that there's not a railwayman alive in my generation that didn't see Dautry in flesh and blood at least once.

He worked for the railways 24 hours a day and nothing got past him. He'd always get to the bottom of things, he'd appear without warning and sort out even the smallest problem. However, he expected the same dedication from his subordinates. His favourite saying was: 'Sanctions go according to rank.' If a lamp man commits an error he should be reprimanded, but it was only fair that if a more senior employee does something wrong, the sanction should be more severe.

In 1930 he showed up at Saint-Mariens. He came on his special train with all the Paris officials and those from the Saintes region. He began with a meticulous inspection of the loco sheds but overall he didn't find anything out of line. The Saint-Mariens station too was impeccable. The signals were like new and it was clear that doors, windows and even the sleepers had been repainted. He was so impressed that he asked the station master and deputy if it was always so well kept. Obviously they said yes. But as he was getting in his car to leave he saw some children playing football. By the strangest of coincidences the ball landed right at his feet and one of the kids ran up, apologised and picked up the ball.

'Tell me,' said Dautry to the young lad, 'is the station always as neat as this?'

'Don't be silly. They're expecting the Director. They've been at it a week!'

Turning towards his staff he said, 'You see gentlemen the truth always comes from the lips of a child.'

When he got to Blaye, he inspected the goods hall, the dock facilities then the passenger station. As was his custom, he then went to the guard room, which was for the traction crews and train staff, to see the state of the plates and cutlery as well as the sleeping accommodation for the crews. He pulled out chipped, broken and cracked bowls and pans hardly worthy of the name. Everything was as old as the hills. In a real temper he sent for the station master responsible:

'Would you eat off a plate like this at home?' he railed.

'Of course not *Monsieur le Directeur*,' answered the station master lowering his head.

'My men aren't dogs! They work long hours and they've got the right to eat off a clean plate like anybody else.'

He was so annoyed that he smashed the whole lot there and then.

'You've got till this evening to replace this lot. Now jump to it!'

'Yes *Monsieur le Directeur*,' said the station master sheepishly.

For Dautry, the men's well-being was sacred and he spared nothing. He had no time for favouritism nor contempt for the more junior administrative workers.

A good few of the men at the main loco depot at Montrouge Chatillon lived in the Paris suburbs and had often asked for the guardhouse and canteen to be extended or better still, a new complex built. The Director had, of course, acceded, since he thought their request only fair. At the end of 1930 he visited Montrouge accompanied by his secretary. It was 12.30 and the men were on their lunch break. He used the opportunity to look over the depot, the clerk's office, the repair shop and the guardhouse. He then decided to call in the *bureau d'ordres* and was surprised to see four or five staff who, keeping to their old habits, refused to eat in the guardroom canteen.

'What are you doing here?' asked Dautry sharply.

'We're having our lunch Sir,'

'Get out of this office at once! You ask me for a new canteen and you don't even use it! It's absurd. I suppose you fat-arsed pen pushers don't see yourselves next to the workers eh? I don't want to see you scoffing in here again, d'ye hear? Everyone eats in the canteen. No exceptions.'

With that they picked up their plates and scuttled out without another word.

He didn't hesitate to take the initiative when any kind of professional abuse occurred. One day apparently, he took the local train, alone, just like an ordinary passenger and got off at a small Normandy station. There was one railway official on the platform.

'Are you the station master?'

'No, I'm his assistant.'

'Can you tell me where your boss is then?'

'Don't know, I'm afraid.'

'But he's at work today?'

'Yes; but why all the questions, what do you want anyway?'

'My name's Dautry. I'm the Head of the State Railways,' and on seeing his card the assistant turned pale.

'I'll get him for you, Sir!'

The Director's eyes followed him as he left the station and crossed the road to a small café where the station master was engaged in a game of cards. It's possible that Dautry had come especially to catch him in *flagrant délit* . What's more he detested alcoholism and he fervently wished to rid management of this vice. He went with the offender into the station office to give him a dressing down.

'So you were in a bar while on duty. That's a serious offence that warrants serious punishment. You will get a severe reprimand from my office, a last warning and lose ten months of your twelve month year-end bonus.'

Then he asked how many children he had and rounded the sermon off with some moral advice.

'You could at least think of them. I hope you've learnt your lesson.'

Every Saturday Dautry called the managers of the various services to a meeting. On the Saturday following his Normandy visit he told the story to a highly attentive audience.

'I wanted to make an example,' he said.

All the service chiefs nodded in agreement, but were surprised when Dautry continued.

'However, gentlemen, ever since the event I've had a troubled conscience. Losing just about all your annual bonus when you're on a modest station master's wage makes a big difference. I fear that in fact it's his children who will suffer at Christmas. What's your opinion gentlemen?'

His men repeated that an example had to be made and, after all, it was an open and closed case. After a few moments though Dautry gave his decision.

'No. It's not possible for us to punish the innocent. The station master's bonus will be docked but the Social Club has funds for Christmas presents for the needy if I remember right. *Monsieur chef de Service*, make sure his children get something.'

The whole room agreed it was a lesson in initiative. That was Dautry for you.

Anyway, back to 1929 when Dautry started as Director. He attacked the issue of the CIMT workshops in Saintes. He saw clearly that the quality of the work wasn't up to scratch. I'm not saying there was deliberate sabotage but the search for speed and savings left a lot to be desired. Dautry brought government pressure to bear on the affair by reducing the lease on the workshops from fifteen to ten years. This meant that suddenly the CIMT had only a few months left before the lease finished and they would have to get out.

But the decision posed serious problems for the 2,000 workshop employees. Three quarters of these were former employees of the old Paris-Orleans-Midi Railway Company (PO) who had lost their jobs after the 1920 strike and many of these were from Perigord. In 1924 the *Cartel des Gauches* [8] had taken back the workers from the state service who had been sacked, but had been unable to do anything for the PO men in the private sector. These workers had found work in the CIMT but had to follow the company, since the it was using the shutdown to transfer its different departments. The coach shop

---

(8) The government majority of ten left-wing parties elected in May 1924 as a reaction against the *Chambre Bleu Horizon* of 1919.

was to go to Mantes and the engine shop was to be split between Marseilles and Givors.

However, the workers from Saintes weren't too happy at leaving their homes and relations behind. Dautry's approach to the delicate issue was to receive a delegation of all categories of personnel in early April. I was chosen to represent the former apprentices and I turned up one morning at the workshop office. I waited outside with the other reps and then followed them in when we were called. The Director faced us.

He wasn't a very tall man. He had brown hair and a small moustache but the most striking aspect was his eyes. They were bright and sharp. He spoke to us for about three quarters of an hour explaining why he wanted to put the workshops in the State network. His voice and his arguments were so clear he could well have been a lawyer rather than our Director. He immediately put us at ease, asked us for our comments then promised to consider any suggestions or demands.

The decision was that the former PO employees would follow the CIMT as planned, but he promised to do his utmost to ensure that the Saintes workers kept their jobs in the workshops when they were transferred to the State and to decide every case on its merits. When it was my turn he asked me who I represented. 'The old CIMT apprentices set up after the 1920 strike.'

'It makes no difference to me if you're before or after 1920. It's the government that financed your apprenticeship at college with the aim of having professionals in the service. Have you made an application to join the State network?'

'Yes Sir.'

'Then make another. Address it to me personally. I'll be needing men at the end of the year. The other former apprentices will get priority.'

And so I went back to work with high hopes but there was less and less work by the day. Obviously, since the government would be taking over the workshops, the rail network preferred to postpone any work that could wait and so its orders to CIMT dwindled. In October I was shifted from the engine shop to the coach shop which was due to close in only six months. One day I was cornered by the workshop manager. He had a glass eye and was nicknamed 'The Eye of Moscow'.

'Right Péroche, listen to me. If you want to keep your job you'll have to move to Mantes like the rest of us, otherwise you're out.'

Obviously I said I'd go with the CIMT, hoping that Raoul Dautry would get me into the new State workshops before that happened. But would he keep his word?

I was in a tricky situation and the future wasn't certain at all. Yet it was just then that Antoinette and I decided to get married. Since my return from Algeria I continued to see Antoinette but without making any plans because I felt it was too early to think about starting a home. As for Antoinette, however, she became increasingly keen on the idea.

In July 1929 I was invited to her younger sister's wedding.

'Look how happy they are,' she said to me.

So that was it. On 14 September, the same year, we tied our destinies together. Some say that marriage is just a lottery. If that's the case I reckon I've won the jackpot a few times over.

At the end of November I burnt my hand quite badly in the forge and to make matters worse it became infected. I was off work, recovering from the accident when I received a letter with the heading *Reseau des Chemins de Fer de l'Etat, rue de Rome, Paris*. I was invited to sit the entrance exam in Saintes and have a medical. If both of these went well I'd then be asked to take an aptitude test. I set off to see my old doctor and explained the situation.

'I'm a bit worried about my hand, doctor. Do you think I'll get through the medical?'

'If I was in their place I wouldn't worry about your hand, as long as the rest was all right. But will you be able to do the practical? That's the problem.'

Finally I decided to take my chances. I had the opportunity to get into the railways and it wasn't the moment to start feeling sorry for myself. I passed the exam, then the medical.

All that was left was the practical. I wasn't worried since all they wanted was a dovetail joint which I'd done plenty of times when I was an apprentice. While I was doing my test in the machine room I saw the boss walk by. I was sure he saw me with his one eye that saw everything, but he didn't say anything.

A while later when my hand had healed I booked into the coach shop at seven as usual. At half past seven I was summoned to the Eye of Moscow's office.

'Péroche,' he said, 'as we said, you'll be coming to Mantes with us and . . .'

It was pointless letting him carry on and there was no point in lying since he'd seen me taking the practical. I explained my application to work in the State Railways. He was livid.

'Very well. Get your tools. And you see that space in the wall where they've forgotten to put any bricks? Get yourself through it. And good luck to you on your damned railways!'

I thanked him and went through the aperture he had indicated.

I learnt that I'd passed the aptitude test but had no idea when I would be offered a job. Getting laid off just after getting married made it all the more worrying since Antoinette's wages didn't amount to much. For the moment we lived with my parents but that couldn't last forever.

As luck would have it, however, one Sunday morning at six the postman left a letter I recognised immediately. I ripped it open and unfolded the letter. 'Monsieur Péroche, you have been appointed to the depot at Montrouge-Chatillon in the assembly-adjusting department as from 1 February 1930.'

I was expecting everywhere except Paris. My wife was absolutely delighted at the idea of moving to the capital but as for me, I pondered the fate of my rugby.

The same day, after a championship match against Rochefort, I told the managers my news. They were disappointed that I'd have to leave. At the annual club dinner, not long after at the Couronne restaurant, we had two guests of honour: the mayor, Fernand Chapsal and the local deputy, Maurice Palmade. At the end of the meal they both mentioned how sad they were at losing me but promised that once I'd finished my apprenticeship, they'd do their best to get me back to Saintes.

I had only a few days left with Antoinette since I'd have to find lodgings before she could join me. For the first time in my life, I was on my way to the City of Light.

A Pacific approaching a signal gantry at Chartres
circa 1930 (Collection Viollet)

CHAPTER 2
A Year in Paris

AS SOON as I arrived in Paris, I made my way to
Montrouge, along with my friend from Saintes, who had
been passed the same time as me. We had before us one of the
most famous and modern depots in France. The Pacifics waited
in the roundhouse, steamed and ready to go, like racehorses at
the starting gate. Twenty four hours a day these steel monsters
crisscrossed the whole of France.

We had the first day off to find lodgings. I found a room
near the depot easily, on the Chatillon road near the Bagneux
cemetery. By sheer coincidence, the couple who ran the
boarding house were from Saint-Dizant-du-Gua, in the
Charente – my father's birthplace!

When we booked in the next day at seven, we were put on
two different maintenance crews. I got into the swing of things
quite quickly, since I had done some time in the Saintes'
workshops. I enjoyed the work. The tools and equipment were
modern and the atmosphere of camaraderie much warmer than
at Saintes. I was keen to get some permanent lodgings so that I
could bring my wife and after a great deal of searching I found
a room with a bed, a table, four chairs plus electricity. There
was a small stove, which provided for both heating and
cooking. Also, we could also use the small garden at the front
of the house. The rent was 250 francs and I earned only 1,025.
Still, my mind was made up and I went to get Antoinette at
Saintes.

For her too, Paris was completely new. We knew nobody
and were absolutely lost in the enormous place. But our spirits
were high. I was paid fortnightly before being commissioned
and we only had meat and wine for a few days after my wages

came in. When the money ran out we seemed to love each other more. Bad times, as they say, always make the good times seem better.

One day the Director, Raoul Dautry visited the Montrouge depot. I was adjusting the wheel bearings on a Pacific when he walked down the centre of the workshops alongside the *chef de dépôt* and our foreman. Suddenly he left the two men he was with and made his way towards me.

'Don't I know you?' he asked. 'Of course! You're the apprentice at Saintes.'

I was dumbfounded that he should remember me. He asked me how long I had been at Montrouge, whether I liked the work and what were my plans for a career.

'The future's ahead of you. If you work hard, we'll look after you. You've two choices. Either you can become a *chef d'équipe* or even a foreman, there are schools for that. Or you can go for train crews – as for those, I want real professionals.'

'I rather fancy the second.'

'Very well,' he said, smiling at me.

He tapped my shoulder amiably and went off with his managers. As soon as he had gone my work mates were at me.

'How do you know Raoul Dautry then?'

In order to satisfy their curiosity I told them of my meeting in Saintes as a representative of the apprentices.

In the meantime, my wife had found a job with a cousin from my father's side. She ran a small business along with her husband, an Auvergnac, tailoring trousers. Antoinette had never worked in this line before, but as she was deft with her fingers, they gave her a try. She walked three kilometres, four times a day to get to Malakoff, which wasn't served by the metro in those days.

Like any Auvergnac worth his salt [1] he wasn't a generous

---

(1) Southern Auvergne is a predominantly rural region and experienced massive emigration to Paris. Consequently, the 'Auvergnacs' had a very thrifty approach to life.

boss, but beggars can't be choosers and we were glad of the little extra.

Later, she found work as a seamstress in the Rue de Rivoli, thanks to a friend of one of her uncles in La Rochelle. It was better paid and she got a meal at midday, but most of all, the journey to work took far less time since she could take the metro or the train. Our situation improved and occasionally we went to the cinema or even a restaurant on some Sundays. We used to get a good meal for 6 francs at the Mille Colonnes, Rue de Gaîté in Montparnasse.

In June 1930, five months after being taken on, my life took a new turn. I was just back from a visit to my parents in Saintes and was in the inspection pit alongside two colleagues from the maintenance team. We were busy fitting the leaf springs over the driving wheels on a Pacific when the foreman came up. He was a fine figure of a man, impeccably coiffed and always wearing his black hat. At that time all those with any rank sported a hat to show their status and bolster their authority.

'Who wants to get on the footplate?' he asked. 'There are more than a hundred extra trains running at the end of the month [2] and the allocation office needs more men.'

As no-one volunteered, he nodded towards us three and told us to sign up. He was perfectly entitled to do this since all workers in the railways sign a clause in their contract to say that they will work on engines when necessary.

Despite a certain anxiety I was happy to have been ordered on train crews. I handed in my tools and made my way to the allocation office. There I found the *sous-chef de dépôt*, looking immensely sombre in his black jacket and inevitable black hat.

'Name? Address? Stay at home, that's an order!'

'But . . . er . . . I've only just started Sir! I haven't actually done any service on an engine . . .'

'Sort that out like the rest have to lad. Go home and don't leave the house.'

---

(2) These were the additional summer holiday specials.

Antoinette was surprised to see me back home at four in the afternoon.

'What's happened?'

'Nothing. But as from tomorrow, I'm on the footplate.'

The next day at around eleven a call boy arrived at the house. His job was to call up train crews when they were needed. I knew him from our school days in Saintes. He handed me a work sheet to man one of the Montrouge-Montparnasse shuttle services between eight at night and four in the morning. These ran every hour or two and meant that the railway workers wouldn't have to wait for the suburban trains. Moreover, they went directly to the Montrouge depot, thus saving time. During the day, they carried ordinary rail workers, administrative staff and supervisors, but at night they were used almost exclusively by train crews and night watchmen. They were made up of five coaches and a fairly dated engine, usually an 0-6-0, which meant a locomotive with six driving wheels and no leading or trailing bogie.

To get to Montparnasse station from Montrouge, where I had to relieve the fireman, I was told to catch a ride on an engine from the Thouars depot which was to leave Montrouge at 7.15 to head the Bordeaux express. I was really impressed since it wasn't just any old engine, it was one of the most up to date, superheated Pacifics. I explained my situation and asked the driver if I could join him in the cab.

He gestured me aboard. He was a large, kindly man with a blue driver's cap, a sun visor hanging round his neck, like those the cyclists use in the Tour de France and, of course, the inevitable pair of goggles.

It was warm outside, so next to the fire door it must have been 50^0 and there was a strong smell of hot lubricating oil. The tender carried about eight tons, made up of good quality coal and briquettes, sometimes known as bricks. Five or six tons would be used over the 330 kilometers between Paris and Thouars.

The signal dropped and the powerful beast eased forward as if it could hardly wait to be moving. A few hours later it would be running at 120 kilometres an hour – but with 500 tons behind it. The engine moved onto the main line and slipped through the West Circular. To left and right, suburban trains scurried by. It seemed impossible to know what was happening. The driver stayed relaxed. He'd come gently to a halt in front of stop signals and then pull away smoothly when they changed. How on earth did he know which ones were for him? When I saw the bank of colours – white, red, orange and purple – I thought I'd never master such a job.

The fireman opened the firebox door to stoke up.

The famous spy in the cab

Thick smoke mixed with enormous flames spewed out, reaching right to the back of the cab.

'See that?' he said. 'There's a ton of fuel in there. Bricks and coal – so as to get a good fire bed.'

The driver took his rag to wipe the brass-rimmed gauges for the steam pressure and the water reserve as well as the Flamann Band reader. [3] Everything that could be polished shone like a new pin.

'It's the finest job there is lad,' said the big fellow, 'but you have to like it. You have to take it seriously; learn your rule book and regs and you'll be a driver one day. You'll head the fast trains and make money a-plenty.'

I nodded, but inside, I knew that a lot of water would flow under the bridges of the Seine before that happened.

At Montparnasse the locomotive backed up to the train it would haul. I took my leave of the Thouars crew as the engine was coupling up. The driver clasped my hand for a second or two and then said, 'I wish you the best of luck, lad.'

I thanked him and would never have thought that six years later he'd be my *chef mécanicien* at the Thouars depot.

I now had to find my famous *navette* which was hidden

---

(3) An instrument similar to the black box used to record the speed of a locomotive and the position of signals passed by the driver on a special band of paper. It was invented by Eugène Flamann in 1889 and known by drivers as *le mouchard* or 'spy in the cab'.

among all the other regular and extra trains. Alone in a sea of rushing passengers I searched and searched, but in vain. In the end I spotted the white cap of the *sous chef de gare,* who dispatched the trains. I asked him where my shuttle was.

'How the hell should I know where your shuttle is lad. I've got more than workers' trains to worry about.'

I finally found it parked at one of the suburban line platforms. The driver had left, but the fireman was still in the cab, waiting for the relief crew. He seemed to be a nice fellow so I explained my situation. 'I don't know a thing about the job,' I blurted out.

'That's bad luck mate, 'cos the driver you've got won't be the one to tell you much. He's past retirement age. He's a bloody minded character and neither crews nor bosses have got a kind word for him.'

My morale hit rock bottom.

'Climb up anyway mate,' the fireman continued, 'I'll give you a few tips. First you've got to know how to work the injectors to get water into the boiler, see?'

I knew them well since I had repaired all the controls at the workshops. I learnt how they were used in a flash.

'Good. Now I'll show you how to look after your fire. You don't just sling coal into the firebox any old how. The coal's got to be spread lively like. Don't cram it in, spread it, scatter it and make sure you keep the sides well covered. Rule number one: make sure your fire bed's built like a bird's nest.'

Naturally, my arms were too taught and it took me a while before I got the touch. Then he showed me where the steam draught [4] was located. This was always known as the fireman's mate since it automatically boosted the fire.

Then my fireman left me to it.

---

(4) This control regulates the contact of the exhaust steam with the combustion gases. This could be increased to provide the equivalent of bellows for a domestic fire by pulling more air through the fire bed. It was used when a short period of additional steam was needed (e.g. going up a gradient).

I'd barely lost sight of him when my partner appeared and I knew at once what the fireman had meant. He must have been sixty at least, unshaven with a gray moustache. He wore an old blue cap and greenish overalls with no buttons. I introduced myself but he didn't deem to give a reply.

'It's my first time on an engine,' I explained.

'That's not my problem. I'm not here to teach you, I should be retired by now.'

On these encouraging words, he opened the steam valve and told me to reset the Flamann band. The steam pressure was fine at 12 kilos and the glass water gauge was three quarters full. In other words, we were ready to go.

We got the whistle and the flag and as soon as we were out of the station we were on the main Paris-Chartres line. The locomotive was elderly and the five coaches behind were more than enough. We'd have to keep the pressure up at all costs if we were to avoid stalling on the main line and hold up suburban and through trains. After two kilometres we had already lost a kilo of steam. The fire wasn't bright enough and the engine was sluggish. Still, we managed to climb to the junction at the Montrouge plateau and then backed onto the branch line to the depot. There was only 10 kilos of steam now and a centimetre of water in the glass. It hadn't been brilliant on the climb, but it hadn't been a disaster either.

Thanks to the steam draught and a few stiff rakes of the fire bed the pressure gauge climbed back up. I opened the injectors and refilled my boiler. My partner gave neither praise nor criticism.

Half an hour later we were on the down run to Paris with the engine in front this time. It was easier going, since as everyone knows Paris lies in the centre of a basin. All lines converging on Paris, therefore, go slightly downhill for the last 10 or 15 kilometres. Consequently, the shuttle arrived in better shape in Paris than she'd arrived at Montrouge. With experience as my tutor I made progress on the next run. My fire was brighter and I didn't spare the rake.

At Montrouge we parked for a two-hour break. My partner

Greasing the connectiong rods and especially checking the axle boxes was the driver's responsibility alone
(La Vie du Rail)

went back to the leading coach for a snooze. I stayed alone in the cab and ate a pinch of bread. I was disillusioned and didn't have much of an appetite. Then, while the old timer snored away, I practiced shoveling movements to get the right swing and I brought my coal forward.

At around 2.30 in the morning, the points man gave us a signal with his lamp to leave with the next shuttle. I went to wake up the driver and was rewarded with a few grunts. I opened the steam for the air brake pump and reset our 'spy in the cab'. Before setting off my partner stretched his arm behind the steam intakes and pulled out a canteen filled with coffee. He drank his ration and held it out to me.

'Here, drink that; it'll do you good.'

When I refused, he became annoyed.

'Listen, I give the orders on this engine. When I say drink, you drink.'

To avoid any further trouble, I took a swig. It must have been a quarter rum but after, I realised that it did do me good and more important still, it kept me awake.

At four, after two more runs, our relief crew arrived. My dismal companion at least shook my hand and said, 'See you tonight.'

He had gone up a notch in my estimation.

It was the same scenario, more or less, for the next eight days but with one difference: my confidence went up and so did my morale. My driver was always glum and tight-lipped, but every night, after the break he shared his coffee laced with rum.

At last my rest day came around and as I finished at four in the morning, that meant practically 48 hours of freedom. I used these to visit my parents in Saintes. On my return to Paris, I learnt with relief that I had been taken off the Montrouge-Montparnasse navettes and was allocated to shunting duty at Clamart, which was 7 or 8 kilometres from Paris. The turn was from one in the afternoon to nine at night.

I arrived well in advance and while waiting for my partner,

went to the lamp room to get the head and tail lamps for the special engine used for this service. It was then that I caught sight of a tall, red-faced man bearing down on me. He ambled along slowly, shod in wooden clogs and resembled a stout Normandy peasant. It was my driver. But if 'old grumpy' had hardly said a word, this character more than made up for it. He immediately made me feel at ease.

'Don't you worry young lad, I'll keep you right.'

He showed me how to empty the grate of all the waste and clinker and then how to take water. In between his short lectures he carried out his lubricating round.

At two o' clock we left, engine only, to carry out shunting at Clamart. Before reaching the main line we passed less than 50 metres from my lodgings and I gave my wife, who was looking out for me, a wave. In order to avoid hindering the faster traffic on the main line we ran as fast as we could. Thanks to my Normandy man's advice the steam gauge stayed up. I was in high spirits. I was learning my trade. When my driver saw that everything was running well, he began to tell me about signals. I was all ears.

At Clamart station we were met by the shunting foreman and his team. My partner introduced me to all these fine folk and not long after we started our duties. We had to uncouple some trains and assemble others. Then we were to sort goods wagons, separating those that were loaded and destined for the unloading platforms, ready for reception and those that were empty.

Of course, I didn't yet understand the shunting codes and signals, but the shunter men were very patient and very encouraging. When I booked out on the first night I recognised every sign there was.

Every day at around five in the evening we parked the engine and took an hour's break to eat our sandwiches. This took place in a sort of shelter made out of stacked telegraph poles belonging to the French Post Office where there was enough room for a table and some benches. On my first day I brought some bread and sausage and was ready to get tore into my food when the foreman pulled out a bottle of Dubonnet from behind a pile of logs. This was followed by a respectable bottle of Bordeaux.

'My! my!' I exclaimed, 'I'd never have thought there was such a fine wine cellar in this sort of place.'

The explanation wasn't long in coming.

'The railway's customers always send a case or two of this delicious nectar as a present to the staff. And as we are a cultivated crew with a fine palate we keep the finest here, rather than at home. That keeps our spirits up, as it were, during our breaks.'

The evening finished, therefore, on this happy note. On the return trip I gave a long whistle as I passed our house so that the wife could put on the dinner. She let me know she'd heard by giving me a big wave back. Returning to the depot, my partner showed me how to put the fire on reserve, ready for the next day.

The good life continued through the summer with shunting duty at Clamart and sandwiches with fine vintages at 5 o' clock. Antoinette continued her seamstress days and since I was on engine rosters I got two or three hundred francs more a month. On Sundays we'd visit Versailles, Les Invalides or the Eiffel Tower or sometime go to Colombes stadium for the athletics. After, it was dinner at the restaurant.

On top of this, I had the good luck to have a kindhearted partner who became a bosom friend.

'Tell the wife to get the meat for a *pot-au-feu*,' [5] he said to me one day.

Seeing my perplexity, he continued, 'You can come and get the vegetables. I've got an allotment. You can take a cabbage, some turnips and carrots and a few leeks. I've got the lot!'

Consequently, thanks to our Normandy friend, *pot-au-feu* became a weekly treat.

But all good things must come to an end. September saw the close of summer rosters. There were less trains and extra

---

(5) Traditional French dish made with a variety of vegetables and different meats.

hands were needed to nurse the engines after the punishment of the summer months. Like all the stand-ins, the maintenance workers were taken off the engines and sent back to the workshops. It was with a heavy heart I bade farewell to my delightful cab companion, not to mention the sandwich breaks and the fine wines.

From then on, it was 7 o'clock every day; always the foreman looking over your shoulder and more importantly: less money. However, I looked at it another way. True, I was only a railway worker, not even qualified yet, but there was always the future.

At the same time as this, I had the pleasure of playing rugby again. It was a day in September when I received a letter from the secretary of the Railway Men's Sports Association. I was invited to join the training sessions every Sunday at nine on the playing fields at Saint-Germain-en-Laye. I was also told to bring my wife along as there would be a picnic after training. On arrival at the pitch the secretary greeted me warmly.

'We got to hear you were working in the Paris region. Let me introduce you to the other officials and the players.'

The training and the picnic after took place in an extraordinary atmosphere, as if we were all joined under the sign of friendship. I made friends on the spot, one of whom also played on the wing. He hailed from Beziers, the capital of the game. Perhaps the friendship was a result of our position – I played left wing and he played right!

Our wives became such close friends they were almost never apart.

Our two new friends weren't married, but the birth of their child made them take the vow in front of the mayor and I was to be witness. The wife's maiden name was de Mille and she insisted that the famous American film director was none other than her uncle. Her mother had married the brother of Cecil de Mille in America. However, he had since died, or they'd been divorced and she had returned to Paris.

Once we started playing matches, training was on

Wednesday nights at nine in the goods reception hall at Saint Lazare. The ground was hard but the hall was well lit. After training, bosses and workers alike took a unity drink at the anti-alcohol hall in the Rue Amsterdam. This was because the Director of the Railways, Raoul Dautry, was against meeting up in bars. There were one or two players who didn't work on the railways and we played in the Ile de France second division championships. However, we also played outside Paris, thanks to our rail passes which gave us free, reserved second-class rail travel.

During the 1930-31 season I remember playing in Le Havre, Thouars, Verdun, Rennes, Clermont-Ferrand and Toulouse. I recall playing my first away match in Tremblade, not 40 kilometers from Saintes and a place I'd never set foot in. This was because it was usually the third division teams that played the 'oyster catchers' as they were known as. But it was strange to have left to live in Paris only to end up playing your nextdoor neighbours.

We spent two nights on the train, but on the Monday our turn started at seven and we had to be on form for the job. When he saw me come in worn out, the foreman, who wasn't interested in sport, would regularly give me really tiresome tasks.

'Here comes the ball chaser,' he'd say. 'Well you can mount those leaf springs or reassemble the superheaters, that should do you good.'

It was of little use to complain to the union rep, since work always came before pleasure. Those were the rules and it was fair enough to have to live with them.

This said, it wasn't only tiredness that the away games caused. The first match at Tremblade put me on the horns of another dilemma. Since the Thursday before the match my wife had been suffering from a sore throat. Her temperature rose and an abscess swelled up. It was impossible to leave her alone in the house. On the other hand, what about my very first away match with my new club? Moreover, the team managers lived some fifteen kilometres away; it wouldn't be easy warning them of my absence.

'On you go,' insisted Antoinette, 'Don't worry. You have to be at the match.'

It was in the days before the State Health Scheme and we dithered before sending for a doctor. When the landlord's wife called in, I told her of my dilemma.

'Go on, Mr. Péroche,' said the kind hearted Breton, 'Put your mind at rest, I'll get the medicine and look after her.'

I didn't know how to thank her. I left Antoinette with tears in my eyes to get the last train at eleven o'clock at Montparnasse. My conscience bothered me for the whole journey.

At six on the Monday morning, I rushed up to her room to see how she was. I was relieved to see her with a smile.

'I feel better,' she said.

On a November Sunday the match against the 'Blood and Gold' Paris team went badly for me. The team was mostly made up of Perpignan players who had a reputation for playing rough – hence the name. In the second half, after a particularly brutal tackle by the Catalan full back I got up with a searing pain in the left shoulder. There was no doctor on the sideline and so I resigned myself to the pain. That evening I had dinner with my right-winger friend, but I went home early as the pain worsened and my temperature rose.

After a very bad night I went to the doctor at the Montrouge depot who promptly sent me off to the surgeon at Saint Lazare. The X-ray showed that I had a fractured shoulder costing thirty days off work. But how could I remain a month without pay, since I didn't have enough years in the service to entitle me to sick leave? By sheer good fortune the club officials did the necessary to ensure I remained at work until I was better. It was the left clavicle that was fractured and so I could write without a problem and so I was posted to the *bureau d'ordres*.

A few days later, the *chef de dépôt* said to me, 'Come into my office Péroche, I've a job for you.'

He set me down at a small table next to him and since I

had been a good drawer at school he asked me to make some diagrams from his notes. I had also to answer the phone when he was out. This ample fellow, with a reddish, easy going face sported a black bowler hat and smoked a pipe from morning 'til night. He also had a soft spot for a Pernod and he'd nod at the bottle and say:

'That's what keeps me going you know. It can't do you any harm eh?'

We soon became friends and he'd share his plans for the future.

'I was in charge of the Rochelle depot before here at Montrouge. If you only knew how I miss the Charente. But I'll tell you one thing, I'll retire at either Chatillon or Royan.'

The days went by and my shoulder mended. A really special event was planned for the end of year festivities between Christmas and the New Year. The Paris Railway Men's rugby team had a fixture for two matches in Hanover in Germany. Our team was to be strengthened by two superb players from the provinces but also by the captain of Bordeaux, André Debons. I knew this international star, who had played for France against Australia, because he came from Saintes and I'd played with him at the local ground between 1920 and 1925. It was he that had trained me up and I'd played alongside him in the first team. He'd left then railways to work in a Bordeaux print shop, but the club officials had got him a special dispensation to play for the railways.

They wanted me to take more time to recover but I had decided to get back to my job in the workshops and more than that, to play a match or two to see if my shoulder had healed. It appeared that the fracture had mended and that I could play with no worries. The only cloud on the horizon was the loss of a week's pay. I was advised to write to Raoul Dautry, who was a sports fan. I was docked seven days but later I received some assistance pay which in fact covered the loss.

The week before we left, Dautry called us to a meeting in the anti-alcohol hall to give us some last-minute advice.

'I am truly sorry not to be able to accompany you as I

would dearly have loved to see our German colleagues. Unfortunately my professional commitments prevent me from going to Hanover and the Regional Manager will have to stand in for me. I've called you all here to say that I want good reports of you all. You are the French Railway's ambassadors in a foreign land. You are to play two matches in Germany. For the honour of France and her Railways you must try your hardest to win – but not by any means. Play fairly and if you lose, then lose like true sportsmen. It is a game and only a game. Gentlemen, I put my trust in you.'

On Christmas Eve I went with Antoinette to her brother's in Bordeaux. I then went straight away to Paris and looked up my friend from Beziers in the Rue de Rennes, then I went at a trot to the Gare de l'Est. In the train that steamed towards Hanover we were twenty players, including twelve from Paris, along with three managers and an engineer in charge of the delegation.

When we arrived at the magnificent Hanover station, we were met by the German team managers and some German railwaymen who welcomed us warmly. A hundred or perhaps a hundred and fifty people then followed us to the hotel and applauded their old enemies who had come that day in friendship. The chairman of the German Rugby Federation sat at our table.

We had the next morning free to visit the town, accompanied by an official from the Federation. Our interpreter was a Frenchman from the Northern Region who had been sent to have a look at the new Kunze-Knorr braking system. His wife, in fact was from Charente, Cognac to be exact.

The first match was against Victoria, Germany's top rugby team. It took place on the Sunday and drew a crowd of 15,000 in the vast stadium. Rugby is not such a popular sport in Germany as it is in France and it was the presence of a French team that had kindled their curiosity. Just before the kickoff André Debons laid a wreath at the tomb of the fallen. It stood at the far end of the stadium and commemorated the German sportsmen killed in the Great War.

The young Péroche in sports outfit (Family collection)

Two of our players were injured in the first half and so we ended the match with only thirteen players. The final score was 9-3 to the Germans, but I had the honour of scoring a penalty, forty metres out and not far from the touchline. I was the first to be surprised, since I'd never managed to score from such a distance out and at such an angle. The German victory was due to their extraordinary physical strength, which was way above ours.

Then it was the reception at the town hall, with all the local authority officials as well as the military followed by a banquet at one of Hanover's finest hotels. There were a hundred or so guests including the players, managers, important people from the German railways, politicians and journalists. The French and German players were seated alternately so that I was next to the German winger who had faced me that afternoon. He was a famous German athlete who formed part of the 400 metres relay team. He didn't manage to get past me during the match however – nor I past him!

The dinner was a success with mountains of sauerkraut and charcuterie washed down with gallons of beer. All that beer was slightly on the common side for the French who scanned the table vainly for a bottle of wine. The atmosphere nevertheless was brotherly and I've still got a warm souvenir of the occasion. At the end of the meal there was a speech from the local councillor which was translated for the head of our French delegation. Then there was a speech in perfect French by the burgomaster. He reminded us that he was a First World War survivor and that he had witnessed first hand the courage of the French. He finished with a comment on the war.

'How happy it makes me to welcome you today in my town. My dearest wish is that from this day on, the youth of France and the youth of Germany shall meet only on the sportsfield and never on the battlefield!'

The audience rose to its feet as one and applauded to the roof beams these marvellous words without suspecting how disastrously wrong was our burgomaster's prophecy.

The next day everyone wished to meet the French – from the War Veterans' Association to the Peace Movement, not to mention the Pacifists, a Human Rights group and former prisoners of war. As we couldn't be everywhere at the same time we split into three groups. One group I was in met in the cellar where the beer flowed like water. We were invited to sing but were not up to the gusto of our hosts who were, nevertheless, a lot older than us. They had experienced the war but we felt they were happy to be in our company.

On leaving the beer cellar I noticed on a well-lit wall some giant posters announcing 'A major meeting of the National Socialist Party with the participation of Adolf Hitler, Rudolf Hess, Hermann Goering, Ribbentrop and Goebbels.' These posters meant nothing to me, because at the time Germany was a Republic governed by Chancellor Bruning. An old German came up to me and pointed at these portraits. I write the words he spoke: 'Look there young man! If those characters ever get into power, there'll be another war.'

At the time I took him for a fool, but time has shown that he was a better prophet than the burgomaster. I recalled his sad foreboding more than once during the war.

Our second match was on the Wednesday against an international selection. As with the first it was played in a vast stadium and as with the first there was a giant ceremony with national anthems sang with dignity and a large and orderly crowd. We'd no wish to lose a second time, but our forwards were mauled by the international players. On the other hand, the French backs shone and drew applause from the crowd. In the end all were happy with a 3-3 draw. The evening ended at two in the morning with yet another banquet, uninterrupted singing and an enormous binge – with only beer of course.

Then, the day after, it was off to Berlin, the capital of greater Germany. Our international travel permits allowed for twenty-five visitors when in fact we were only twenty-four. Consequently we could invite one more person. Our hotel owners were a model of kindness and had a pretty, 18 year old daughter as blonde as a Beauce cornfield. When she was serving our breakfast the following morning she said absent mindedly, 'How fortunate you are to be visiting Berlin. I've never been there you know.'

'Fancy coming with us?' asked our engineer.

'I'd love to!' she answered, lowering her eyes shyly.

Our engineer promptly asked her parents' consent who gave it without the slightest worry about leaving her with twenty-four healthy young French men. Everything went swimmingly of course, since Dautry had said that we were the 'foreign ambassadors of the French Railways.'

It had snowed all night and we crossed the countryside blanketed in white The reception and lunch were held at the station buffet where we had the pleasant surprise of a bottle of white German wine. We were then given a guided coach tour of Berlin's monuments including the famous Brandenburg gate and from there to the French Embassy. We were impressed by how clean the city was, but it did not match the beauty of our capital. The evening saw us at the opera house which was one of the world's finest. We had hardly taken our seats before the murmuring began and the faces turned, 'They're the Frenchmen, you know!'

The evening was wonderful and finished on a tour of beer cellars which meant that we did not get to our hotel until four in the morning.

On the return run, the beautiful Gertrude took her leave at Hanover, promising never to forget us. At Liege some foolhardy players got off the train to visit the buffet and the train had to leave without them. At 8 o'clock on Friday evening the survivors docked in Paris.

As I was scheduled to play in Rennes on the Sunday, Antoinette was to stay in Bordeaux until the following week. On Saturday I booked in at seven and the first thing I did, along with one of my friends, was to go to the pay officer for a sub since we had returned penniless. We decided to meet in the restaurant at midday when we booked off at eleven. As I was leaving the depot I was surprised to see Antoinette.

'I knew you'd be back,' she said, 'and I couldn't wait.'

It was the purest proof of our love.

'But I'm off tonight to Rennes!'

'I know.'

'Listen, I was supposed to meet a friend in the restaurant but here's some money, buy what you can and cook something for us all. And don't forget the wine!'

While waiting for lunch with Antoinette I caught a drink with my friend and told him of the changed lunch fixture. After the meal Antoinette walked us to the depot where we had a coffee.

Our train left Montparnasse at ten in the evening. Antoinette insisted on seeing me off. When the departure was announced I gave her a kiss before boarding the train and saw the tears in her eyes. 'Alone again until Monday,' she whispered.

It was just then that one of the club officials, who had witnessed the scene, took her arm.

'Come Madame Péroche, climb aboard. Don't worry, we have twenty reservations and only seventeen persons. Your kids aren't expecting you until next week anyway.'

I was speechless. She wiped away her tears and stepped inside. The train rattled through Brittany at 120 kilometres an hour and we both stood cheek to cheek in the corridor. It was a moment of pure happiness.

The match at the stadium the next day was in front of a crowd of 10,000 mainly because we were acting as the prelude for an international football match against Switzerland. By two o' clock the stadium was full, which all goes to show that the townsfolk liked rugby, even in this football heartland.

We won convincingly. I scored two tries, despite my counterpart, who was the French 100 metres champion. Perhaps it was Antoinette's presence that put wings on my heels! Who knows?

My stay in Paris, however, would soon be drawing to a close. In March 1931 a fellow railwayman from Saintes came to see me.

'I know someone who's leaving Saintes if you're interested. Seriously. It's love problems, he wants to leave his wife and come to Paris.'

I got in touch with the man. We both had the same grade, the same year's service and had both finished our probationary periods. Our respective bosses, therefore, had no problem in organising the exchange. On 1 April, after fourteen months away from home, I was put on the Saintes depot payroll.

CHAPTER 3
Life on the Footplate

O N MY RETURN to Saintes I had to make a very important choice between a career as a footplate man or a rugby player. The Saintes club managers had pounced on me like a cat with a mouse and I obviously agreed to put in for a transfer for the next season. But all this was brought into question when the *chef de dépôt* sent for me after two days at work.

'Is it you who's come from the Montrouge depot?' he asked. 'You're a young chap, you should be thinking about getting on the footplate. At the moment I've got thirty or so young lads who are lined up. Ideally, we want young profess-ionals who are looking for a driving career. You seem to have all the paper qualifications, get your application in smartish.'

If I accepted, it was an official commitment. It was a hard choice, since train crews worked nights and Sundays, which meant farewell to any competitions. At twenty-three, I was in good shape for the sport I loved. How could I betray the club managers and the team's supporters?

'Think it over,' advised an old *chef de dépôt*. 'You're at the crossroads. If you're going to work on locos now's the time to move. Just think of the prospects: retirement at fifty with a fair pension. Look here, sports are all very well but it's just a hobby isn't it, after all?'

He sounded sincere and in fact, he was speaking my mind.

'I'll apply,' I told him.

He came up closer and shook my hand.

'Very good lad. You won't regret it.'

I moved to working for the *bureau de feuille*. I spent the first eight days preparing and replacing engines in Saintes station.

Unlike what had happened at Montrouge, I began to learn the basics of the modern engines. These consisted of the Pacifics, taken from the Germans after the First War, 4-6-0s and the works locos left behind by the Americans in 1919.

After about a week I was ordered to pick up a goods train every day at Cognac. It was the perfect exercise for a beginner since it was hauled by an American works loco and halted at every station. My partner showed me how to bank up the fire on this robust little engine. She had a vast firebox and certainly kept her fireman more than busy. Were these Americans some kind of supermen? In any case they were a young race as all their sports' victories showed.

On Easter Monday 1931 I was ordered along with my partner to head a passenger train to Royan. There were crowds of people for the holiday, so much so that the usual loco, a 4-6-0 from the Niort depot wasn't strong enough. Rather than form two trains it was decided for economic reasons to haul the 600 tons with our works engine. Our loco wouldn't go over 70 kilometres an hour, but on the other hand she went up gradients as fast as she came down them. Moreover, we could pull away smartish and this would be useful, since the train stopped at every station.

It was my first train of any size as fireman, but thanks to the advice of the driver, the needle on the steam gauge never wavered and we arrived bang on time in Royan. My partner congratulated me. We grabbed a bite to eat in the guard room and then it was the return to Saintes at the head of a passenger train. Again I kept my fire in good shape and the pressure gauge up. On the platform at Saintes hundreds of passengers streamed towards the exit while I stood on the engine totally exhausted. But I wouldn't have missed that first day for the world.

After this I crewed with a driver who had only recently been allocated a dedicated engine. He was nice enough but as lazy as a dog. He never helped the fireman to take the head and tail lamps back to the lamp room nor give a hand to get the coal forward. Fortunately, I was young at the time and

The 4-6-0
locomotives
were the
passenger
engines 'par
excellence' with
large diameter
driving wheels
to ensure high
speeds
(La Vie du Rail)

never tired, so I took him as he was. Every week we worked the same trains serving Angouleme, Saint-Mariens, La Rochelle and Bordeaux as well as through and local trains to Saint-Mariens. This service lasted until 1932 when I again had to stand down from the engines.

The economic crisis was felt even on the railways, since unemployment and factory shutdowns meant less and less freight. The government under Pierre Laval [1] hoped to redress the situation by a series of decrees, not dissimilar to a dictatorship. He cut wages by 10% for civil servants, teachers, railwaymen, soldiers and the police. There would also be no promotion. I lost three years advancement because of these unpopular measures. More importantly, however, as I was not yet a passed fireman, I had to go back to the workshops.

There the work was slack too, since the drop in traffic

(1) Pierre Laval 1883-1945. Initially a lawyer representing trades union causes Laval's hatred of communism pushed him to the right. His deflationary strategy provoked strong public unrest. He collaborated with Germany during the occupation and was executed in 1945.

entailed a drop in maintenance and repairs. Consequently I was detached from the track service and moved first to electrics and then to technical services. I stayed there a year making adjustments and working in the forge, always with the same partner. We were also involved in the construction of a signal and points box at Royan. We'd often take a packed lunch and eat in the open air. What's more, the Sunday rest day meant that I could take up rugby again with the reserves.

Eventually the economy recovered and the traffic increased accordingly. All the workers who had been stood down were back on the engines. The allocation chief put me on a 4-6-0 number 803 which headed the local trains to Bordeaux, Nantes, Angouleme, Niort and Royan. We also looked after the mixed goods and perishables to Bordeaux and lastly, the Rochelle-Geneva fast train as far as Angouleme. It was the most important service in the department and the one that paid the best wages because it was extremely hard work.

Unlike the Pacifics, the 4-6-0 800 class had a 4 wheel front bogie, six coupled driving wheels but no trailing bogie. They didn't work on superheated steam, which reached 300^0, they simply worked on saturated steam at 100^0. Consequently, these engines needed more water, more coal and more work! Nevertheless, at 25 tons, more or less, they could haul the same as Pacifics.

My partner, Milha, was one of the oldest drivers in the depot and had only two years to go to retirement. He hailed from Perigueux and since he had done his national service in the navy would call his workmates 'seaman' or 'sailor.' He was always to be seen with his sea dog's cap. This gentle, but cocky old fellow was always lying in wait with a good word to say on a bad day and is certainly the most original character I've ever met. When I offered to take him for a coffee he would systematically refuse.

'Chief,' I used to say (he loved being called chief) what about an aperitif?'

'What's that you say shipmate? You're wanting to take me to a place where they swallow your money up and ruin your health?'

He was an excellent driver but because of his constant worries about money could never make up lost time. If he left Saintes five minutes late, he arrived at his destination five minutes late, otherwise that meant 'spending more coal'. He pulled me up more than once on this point. He'd count my briquettes and sometimes he'd shut the firebox door when I was stoking, saying that I'd already put in one shovelful too many. For all that, he was a kind man and he always had a smile.

'Shipmate, we don't work for glory, we work for money!' was one of his sayings.

Once, when our engine was lifted [2] for a month, Milha decided to take his holidays and so I was crewing with all and sundry. It was at this time that I saw Raoul Dautry again, in very unusual circumstances.

Every August there are splendid shows in the Gallo-Roman arenas in Saintes. The Comedie Francaise could attract some 20,000 spectators and was attended by famous people such as Raymond Pointcarré and the like.

In 1934, Dautry came to the festival which included in the programme *Pour la Couronne* starring Maurice Escande. When I was young, I often used to play in the school dramatic society and that year I decided to get back into acting, since I found it relaxing. Robed in purple I had the role of a deacon, which was more decorative than anything. I went to three or four rehearsals before the play because I didn't have many lines in fact. After the play, the Director came up on the stage and, as was customary, shook hands with the players and congratulated the production staff. Dautry recognised me at once.

'What are you doing here?'

'I'm one of the actors Sir, there's no harm in that is there?'

'Not at all!' he said with a laugh.

The very same evening Dautry and his family stayed at Fernand Chapsal's house. He was the Senator-Mayor of

---

(2) When a locomotive is taken to the workshops and lifted so that the wheels and axles can be removed and checked.

Saintes and got on with Dautry's family famously. Raoul Dautry appeared at Saintes station in the morning ready to take the Royan Paris express. He was wearing blue dungarees and a Basque beret. Instead of climbing aboard his personal, white-roofed leading coach, he joined the crew on the footplate and shook hands with the men. The Director of the Railways stood behind the driver and the train set off for the City of Light. Apparently, the driver kept asking if he wanted a seat but the Director always said no.

At Thouars he climbed down and went for a sandwich and a drink while the new loco was coupled up and the compressed airbrake line tested. Then he was back behind the driver.

After the halt at Saumur the train was through to Paris. It was travelling at 120 kph, when suddenly the three men picked up the smell of burning oil. On leaning out, the driver could see that the anti-friction metal on one of the driving wheel axle-boxes had melted. [3] The engine would have to be changed at the next depot; that meant Chateau-du-Loir. The driver gave four long blasts on the whistle in each station he passed so that a request could be telephoned in advance for a reserve loco.

On arrival at Chateau-du-Loir the reserve engine was ready to replace the faulty Pacific. It was a Mikado and its maximum speed was 100 kilometres an hour, which was well below that of the Pacifics. Fortunately, the driver, who I later got to know well at Thouars, was an old timer. Before driving Pacifics he had been a dedicated driver on a Mikado. What's more, he knew the road like the back of his hand.

The engine changeover cost twelve minutes and it would take something special to bring the train in on time at Montparnasse. But the driver had one thing in his favour. The superior power of the Mikados meant they could keep up a speed of 90 – 95 kilometres an hour even when climbing

---

(3) Unlike the driving wheel bearings of a car or electric/diesel locomotive those of a steam locomotive suffered far more stress. This was because the wheels were driven by a longitudinal force from the cylinders, which could reach 100,000 lbsf. When the temperature of the bearing rises above 230^0 the alloy begins to run and the engine has to be nursed to the nearest halt.

The 2-8-2 Mikado was a versatile loco, but with smaller driving wheels and catered for power rather than speed (La Vie du Rail)

whereas the Pacifics would drop to 60, or even 50, on gradients. Since there are numerous inclines between Chateau-du-Loir and Paris a talented driver could snatch back minutes and make up for a delay. When the train pulled into the capital, the Director, the driver and the firemen were as black as jackdaws. Raoul Dautry shook their hands and said to the driver: 'The engine changeover was regrettable, but I must congratulate you on an excellent piece of driving.'

After this he returned to his coach to clean up because, in truth, he didn't look too good. All the local newspapers couldn't stop talking about the story with titles such as 'Raoul Dautry pilots the Royan-Paris Express' and the like.

Several days later the driver received an inquiry form on the axle-box and the melted cover. He could only give the standard reply: 'Routine greasing completed.' He was censured and had a symbolic fine. He was a dedicated driver and therefore responsible for greasing his machine. That's the price and nobody should be offended by it.

So this banal affair appeared to be history when management received a note from Raoul Dautry himself. He wrote: 'The need for an engine changeover for the Royan-Paris at Chateau-du-Loir was regrettable, but I would like particularly to congratulate the driver whose skill allowed us to make up twelve minutes and with a machine of a different type. These congratulations also apply to the fireman whose efforts and courage I cannot praise enough. Consequently, I am allocating to each the sum of . . .' And the amount was exactly the same as the fine!

The driver was punished for a fault for which he was responsible, but his achievement was rewarded. Raoul Dautry had showed yet again his true railwayman's qualities: uncompromising with the rules, understanding of the difficulties of the job and a love for justice.

Our 4-6-0 803 came back from the workshops looking like new. Her steaming had improved and she used less water. Milha was as happy as a sand boy.

'Listen shipmate, we're going to make money with this new engine. A machine like that's better than a woman because she makes money while women just spend it.'

Work was never dull with a character like Milha.

Nevertheless, our partnership only lasted until September 1934. After a morning's work devoted to waxing the boiler and polishing the hoops, I went to eat at the guard house. I wasn't too happy to see that Milha had not even waited for me for lunch. He made fun of polishing and the only thing he asked of me was enough water and steam to haul the Paris-Royan express. He was as cheerful as usual but I was irritated.

Just before pulling into Saujon my injector had failed. One of the joints of the inlet pipe from the tender had come away. No sooner had I noticed this than the safety valves started blowing. For the first time I saw my friend get angry. This was 'expenditure', this meant 'coal was being wasted'.

'My injector's finished,' I said to him, 'use yours.' [4]

---

(4) Injecting water into the boiler as the steam is expended is crucial. However, the system for doing this is complex since the incoming water is injected against the pressure inside the

'No no shipmate, nothing I can do.'

He waited until there wasn't a drop of water in the glass before he released his injector. I don't know what got into me but suddenly I exploded in anger. I told him exactly what I thought of him.

'I've had enough of your daft ideas about saving coal. It's an obsession with you. On top of that you're always saying that you'll give me a chance to drive when we've an easy train; but you've never done it. You've never handed over the regulator, not once!'

At Royan he tried to apologise but I wasn't speaking to him. I was annoyed and set on separation. The next day was my rest day and I used it to go and see the *chef de feuille* and request a replacement. He asked me to think again since my decision irritated him.

'It'll be difficult to find a partner exactly to your taste,' he said sarcastically.

But I stood firm. It was divorce. Sometimes I regretted it because Milha was an honest, cheerful partner and an excellent driver. But on that day he went too far.

I got a new crewman and a new locomotive, an English 2-8-0. She was easier to work, more flexible and better behaved than the works loco. Launay was my new partner. A very decent fellow, from Nantes and only recently dedicated. Although he was only forty, he suffered from poor health with bowel trouble, which often forced him to stop work. Perhaps he wasn't the best engine driver in the world, but he knew his machine inside out. He loved to explain to me how the steam was distributed and he was an excellent teacher, I can tell you. Right from the first day he told me, 'Now you should be learning how to drive a train. Here, take the regulator.'

I was as proud as a peacock. He watched me carefully and was always ready with sound advice. He knew how to make me understand.

---

boiler. Should the nozzle become blocked and the water supply stopped the fire would have to be dropped to avoid pressure building up inside the boiler. It was customary, therefore to fit two injectors to every steam locomotive.

'A touch more speed,' he'd say, 'main regulator now, cut back.'

When pulling into stations he guided my hand to bring up the engine using the driver's brake. [5] He made me drive every day. My confidence grew and soon I could drive and look after the fire at the same time.

It was this skill that allowed me to work my first train as driver. We found ourselves at Chateauneuf-sur-Charente and we were due back at Saintes when my partner was struck down by an attack with his innards. There was no replacement available. Normally I should have asked for a reserve driver but that would have meant a considerable wait and would have upset the traffic flow.

'Don't worry,' I said, 'we're off.'

'You can't. No question about it. It's not allowed,' he answered. But he was in such pain that in the end he let me be. It was a serious infraction, but luckily he had enough strength to keep his eye on me and help me with advice. For me, this run was a moment of joy even more so in that not another soul ever knew about it.

In January 1935, I was invited to take the courses given by the *chef mécanicien* with a view to becoming a passed or qualified driver. For a month I attended the college with twenty or so other workers and firemen. The first week was on signals, the second on general regulations, the third concerned the locomotive and the fourth, the braking system and general maintenance. The state network had only just decided to make this substantial investment rather than leaving us to learn alone. It was our duty to make the best of the opportunity.

The *chef mécanicien* spoke simply and knew how to explain things. When he thought it was necessary he wouldn't hesitate to stop the course and climb onto an engine to make his point clear.

On the last day this is what he said. 'My good friends, we've just spent a month together. The examination's close and will decide your career. In my view, you are all good but you've

---

(5) This was the screw hand brake fitted for parked locos but also a safety brake should the steam/air powered brakes fail.

always got to take luck into account. It's like a bird's nest. Not all the fledgelings survive. There are often some that are snaffled by the cat. Consequently, I wish you all good luck.'

One February morning I was coming back from Saintes after a two day turn when the *chef de feuille* called me. 'You have to be ready for the exam board from eight o' clock on.'

The previous evening I'd been foolish enough to go to the cinema in Angouleme to see *Famille Nombreuse*. I'd not got to bed just before midnight and was up at three. Still orders are orders and it was my turn for the hot seat. I had barely time to wash, put on a change of clothes and get a good strong coffee at the café before turning up at the exam hall at the depot along with a colleague.

The *chef mécanicien* was accompanied by the *chef de dépôt* and the *inspecteur de traction*. They all had long faces since they knew our future was at stake.

My friend was called first and they went over questions that he'd failed the first time around. By half past nine he was home and dry. I went into the office. The session began with signals. For an hour they looked at the subject from every angle and tolerated no hesitation. All three fired questions, but the *chef mécanicien* kept giving me a wink since he really wanted me to pass. After a five minute break it was general regs and safety. 'What do you do when the engine stalls on a gradient? What is the procedure for calling for help from up the line? From down the line?

These questions took up almost an hour, after which we started on the actual locomotive. I felt a lot more at ease on this subject, since it was my strong point. They went on and on about breakdowns and it was clear that they didn't want you to call for a reserve if there was any chance of a running repair. The main thing was to get to the nearest safety station or depot and get off the main line.

Just to show that I knew the practice as well as the theory they took me over to a loco that was steamed. It had gone midday and the workers were coming off shift for lunch. Are these people not hungry? I asked myself. But I had then to suffer the same grilling for the brakes. At last, at twenty to three, we were all four back in the *chef de dépôt's* office.

'Just go into the exam hall and wait,' said the inspector.

After several minutes the door opened and I was gestured to come into the office.

'After due consideration, the exam board declares that Marcel Péroche, railway worker, is fit to drive steam locomotives on the network of the State. You will receive your authorisation from Paris in due course. Prior to this, however, you must drive four test trains. All four count and must be faultlessly driven in the allotted time.'

Two days later I was put in charge of the local Saintes-la-Rochelle train with a 4-6-0 from the Angouleme depot. The dedicated driver travelled in the guard's van while the examining *chef mécanicien* climbed into the cab with me. Everything went swimmingly. We decided to take lunch in a small restaurant since it wasn't the done thing to take a basket with you on a test train.

'Let's take an aperitif,' said the chief. 'A small Pernod wouldn't go amiss.'

In the afternoon I had to take a goods train into Saintes, stopping at every station and carrying out the orders given by *exploitation*. From Rochefort to Saintes I was asked to fire and drive the engine as if the fireman had been taken sick. This was just a formality since very often Launay had been too ill to drive.

The other two tests took place the next day. For the first I was in charge of the Nantes-Bordeaux express headed by a Pacific.

'Don't worry!' said the chief,' She's just like any other loco.'

At Saint-Mariens, I was asked to stop for water. We didn't actually need any water, it was just to see if I knew the procedure. On seeing that I manoeuvred the engine perfectly the chief said to me, 'That's it lad! Lunch time.'

Prior to lunch, of course, we took a small aperitif – not actually laid down in the regulations but necessary, given the circumstances. The last test was to haul train 5924 from Saint-Mariens to Saintes with an English 2-8-0. After a stop at Jonzac for water I arrived at Saintes on time and cock a hoop.

'We'd better drink to that,' said the chief.

A fortnight later I got a letter: 'Railway Worker Péroche is hereby authorised to drive locomotives as a replacement driver.' It was signed by the head of traction and the Network Director.

Thanks to the radical socialist government the block to promotion was lifted and on 1 April 1936 I was posted as passed fireman at Thouars, which was the major depot for the state network outside Paris.

I had to leave my hometown yet again. My family were all over the place although we all worked on the railways. My younger brother was at the Acheres depot after having worked in the Michelin plant. My other brother was not a footplate man but worked on the railway all the same. And my brother in law was to become a foreman at the Saintes workshops.

Thouars is built on the river Thouet and the country around is fairly hilly. It has a population of around 15,000 and is famous for its castle, its viaduct, the Place Laveau and barbecued eels. The local wine is good, since Montreuil Bellay and the famous vintages of Layon are neighbours. Life is pleasant and the locals have an easygoing nature.

At that time the depot was pretty large with 800 employees including office staff. There was also a stack of locomotives: 4-6-0 800s, 4-6-0 300s, 2-8-2s and 2-8-0 500s (known as hunchbacks). There were also a good many 2-8-0 works locos, 0-6-0s and 0-8-0 shunters. But pride of place went to the 4-6-2 Pacifics which headed the Paris-Bordeaux express. In order to work these engines, firemen and drivers alike had to have served their time. The drivers of the Pacifics were known as Senators. They were all on good wages and almost all of them had new houses built to their own plans. It was said that their wives wore silk stockings whereas those of the standard crewmen had to make do with cotton.

We moved in early April to lodgings my wife had found in the town centre, near the Place Leveau. When you arrive at a big depot like Thouars, you are just a face in the crowd and it takes time for you to get yourself a name. My grade as passed fireman allowed me to consider a post on a Pacific one day.

However, most of the positions on the Pacifics were still held by nonprofessionals but who had served their time. Despite the firemen's frustration, the depot chief kept these old timers on *Le Grand Service* and he also held on to his senators – which was only fair.

Consequently, at first I had to settle for a Mikado alongside a quiet and unassuming driver. He asked only that I supply water and steam. I worked the Chartres service with him until he was stood down for health reasons. One afternoon when I was on reserve duty, the call boy brought me an order for the next day written out as follows: 'Peroche, fireman, train 780 Thouars-Paris 4-6-2. Return train 781 Paris-Thouars.' After there was the date and the driver's name. I couldn't believe it. I'd an order in my hand to work an express to Paris on a Pacific alongside a senator. I have to admit that I slept little that night.

I was at the depot very early. I found the engine coaled, the grate clean and the bricks broken up. I went for the head and tail lights at the lamp room and brought them back to the engine. It was then my partner arrived. He carried a large pocket watch the size of an alarm clock on a chain hanging over his plump belly.

'Good morning chief,' I said.

He looked at me without even offering his hand and then grunted something gloomily. My spirits fell. He went off to get his grease from the lamp room and the service sheets from the *chef de feuille's* office. I later found out what he'd said to the *chef de feuille*: 'Who's this character booked on with me? What if he's a good for nothing? I can tell you if she's wanting steam don't count on me to pick up a shovel. You know very well it's a difficult train as it is.'

In fact he was terrified to find himself without his dedicated fireman who had taken two days off. He came back to the engine and got on with his job without giving me a glance. At last we moved out of the yard to couple up to the train. I was careful to make sure the safety valves didn't blow in the station. [6] But deep down I wasn't really worried about this

---

(6) These were fitted to the side of the boiler and would give waiting passengers a shower of boiling steam if they went off next to the platform!

since anyone who has fired a 4-6-0 800 has nothing to fear from a Pacific.

The engine was steaming fine and the water stood at three quarters in the glass. The line is tricky between Saumur and Courtalain, but everything was going a treat. My time-served partner kept an eye on me, but still without a word. All the same, he now looked a little less worried. When he moved to the main regulator to climb the gradients the needle on the steam gauge didn't budge. After a halt at Chartres to take on water we moved on to the main line. The trains from the southwest join those from the west and from Brittany on a common track. The trains, therefore, run quite tightly and it doesn't take much to upset the traffic flow. However, our engine was running at 120 kilometres an hour steady and I'd only touched the rake twice since Thouars.

Around Maintenon a miracle happened. My potbellied partner moved off his post so that he could speak to me.

'Well then laddie, is everything all right?'

'Everything's fine with me. The important question is whether things are all right at your end?'

He moved back to his post and pulled down his goggles, before leaning out and taking the wind full in his face. This he had to do to see the signals which flashed by at the speed we were doing. Then it was Meudon, Vanves, the West Circular and Montparnasse. The train pulled up at the buffers bang on time.

'You'll have to forgive me laddie,' said my partner, lifting off his goggles. 'When I saw you on the engine, I was a bit suspicious. Your age did nothing to inspire me, you know. I've been let down so often by these young bloods that I'm wary now. You'll see when you're a driver.'

We hauled the coaches up to Montrouge and headed back to the guard room to wash up. 'No sandwiches tonight,' he said to me. 'We'll eat out. It's on me.'

He was so insistent I had to give in. We left the depot fresh as daisies without, of course, forgetting a tipple at Bougnate's. The man who I'd taken for a grumpy old bear didn't stop talking all evening. We'd both been mistaken and we've been friends ever since. After a hearty meal we made a round of the big cafés until one in the morning.

The next days after submitting his train papers and traction forms to the clerk he nodded at me and said to the clerk, 'If one day I lose my partner, allocate me this lad.'

'So we'll say no more about the comments you made yesterday on the boy?'

'That's right.' he said, 'I was wrong.'

Unfortunately, I never had the chance to crew with him again. I stayed for a while on a reserve service until a passed fireman moved up to become a trainee driver and freed his place. It was through this that I worked with an exceptional partner. He was a former shunting driver, 45 years old, who had climbed the ranks through merit alone. He loved going out, he was cheerful and was all for a good time. In short he was a bit like me.

Our regular service began at four in the morning with the express Paris-Les Sables-d'Olonne, leaving from Thouars. We used to take our rest day at this beautiful spa before heading the Les Sables-Paris express. We'd stop at Thouars to coal and water and from there take the Paris-La Rochelle express, passing through Bressuire and Fontenay-le-Comte. Therefore it was two hard nights in a row, since the Sables line isn't the smoothest in the world. What's more, we worked a 4-6-0 800 – an engine known to have buried a good few firemen before their time.

Initially I felt that he was uneasy because he didn't know me. He was obviously worried that he'd be forced to drive and shovel coal on an express train, and all in the middle of the night.

'I know these engines,' I said to reassure him. 'I was a dedicated fireman on one at Saintes. She'll steam all right, you'll see.'

All along our first run he never stopped complimenting me.

'I'll keep you lad. As soon as we get back to Thouars I'll put a request in writing.'

It was dawn as we approached Sables. As we neared the station he gave a long whistle.

'Come over here lad,' he said.

I crossed to his side only to see four bare arms – female arms – waving from a window. Above the window you could read the sign 'The Railway Man's Bar.' Before even putting the fire on reserve and bringing my coal forward for the evening I had to follow him to his bar. A delightful girl of around 25 greeted us. She was on the petite side with blue eyes and beautiful brown hair. She looked strangely like the famous actress of the day, Louise Carletti. My partner introduced me.

'Alice, this is my new crewman, all fresh from Saintes. I'm going to ask for him.

'Excuse me a minute,' she said in a hushed voice, 'I haven't had time to make myself presentable. I'm just up to get the coffee on.'

'You couldn't be more beautiful than you are now,' I said.

'Well thank you,' she replied, lowering her eyes.

My partner told me her story later when we were working at the depot.

'She was a widow at 24 but she wanted to carry on with the café. She worked hard. The traction men, workers from *exploitation* and even those from the narrow gauge Vendée train came every day. She'd have made some money if her customers had been honest, but there were a lot who took advantage of her and didn't pay their way. She's a weakness for us black boys and she'll end up unhappy.'

His prediction came true and she was eaten out of house and home. As for the other pair of arms, they belonged to her neighbour who stayed with her when her husband was away. The blast on the whistle had become a habit as had the waves from the window.

The bistro was always crowded and since our Louise Carlatti double also had a beautiful voice we didn't hesitate to ask her for a song or two.

Later, on a Saturday in July, we were officially told that

Raoul Dautry's coach would be added to our train. The Director was going to Meilleraie to visit an SNCF holiday camp and would then leave for La-Roche-sur-Yonnne the following evening.

On the Sunday morning at Sables a man wearing a black jacket, who I seemed to recognise, came over to speak. It was Reynaud, the driver who I'd worked with six years earlier when I had first climbed aboard an engine under pressure before working the ill-fated Montrouge-Montparnasse navettes with 'grumpy'.

Since then he'd worked his way up the ladder and become *chef mécanicien* at Thouars. He recognised me at once.

'Marcel! I'm here to join you this evening on the Sables-Thouars express. It's only normal when the Director takes the train.

Just at that moment, my partner showed up.

'Where are you two eating at midday? Reynaud asked, 'In the canteen?'

As we both kept an awkward silence Reynaud went on, 'Tell the Railway Man's Café to put an extra place setting.'

And so we both rushed off to see Alice to say that there would be a 'one of the bosses' joining us for lunch. She accompanied us to the market while her charming neighbour Jeanne looked after the bistro. It was imperative that such a guest was served an exceptional meal. There's no point in giving details of the menu, save that no speciality was spared. At midday we took our places, all seated 50 centimetres out from the table and all decided that we would not leave until our stomachs touched the edge! The two ladies, as gorgeous as ever, appeared delighted to dine with these knights of the iron road.

After coffee my two friends slept the meal off in preparation for the night's work ahead. As for me, a man of duty, I got back to the engine to prepare the tender. I broke up eighty or so briquettes and mixed them with good quality coal since the train would be a hard haul and the Director would be aboard. I even mixed an extra three tons of coal – just in case.

It was 30⁰ in the shade, I was soaked in sweat and the engine still had to be cleaned. The boiler was under pressure so the heat was intense. Nevertheless I gave her a good waxing and finished off with the Brasso on the hoops.

When he got back after his nap and found our engine gleaming Reynaud spoke.

'Congratulations, although you stopped me from sleeping with the noise of your breaking up your damned briquettes. Come on, I'll buy you a drink – you've earned it.' A good idea too, since I had an incredible thirst.

Before we left Alice prepared three bottles of iced water laced with a glass of Pernod. We placed these in a canvas bag with ice and water which we hung in the shade on the tender. The heavy chain of coaches shuddered forwards and our driver gave his whistle to thank our hostesses for having given us such a splendid day. We made out the waving arms which receded and then disappeared. Already the engine was straining at the harness, the glowing cinders from the chimney sparkled like fireworks in the starry night.

At Roche-sur-Yonne, the Director came to shake hands as he always did, while we took water. Then he did a round of the engine and affirmed that she was clean. then he returned to his coach to continue his talk with his managers. At Thouars our engine was uncoupled and replaced by a Pacific. Being a railwayman through and through, Dautry couldn't resist following the operation closely.

The shed workers turned our 4-6-0 around, pointed her in the direction of Bressuire, then nudged her up to the water column since we would be leaving for La Rochelle at around three in the morning. In the meantime everyone went home and even though it was midnight, Antoinette was waiting up for me. I had a bite to eat while she prepared my bag for the coming 24 hours, then I must have slumped my head on the table for a catnap. Antoinette wasn't for going to bed until she'd seen me off. Just before I left she brewed a strong cup of coffee and then we parted. All that was left for me to do was to clean out the slag, empty the ash pan, take on water and stoke up before we were off to Rochelle.

We had a spell of fine running with no hitches whatsoever until one day my friend Reynaud had a serious problem. In fact he had managed to charm the young Jeanne, Alice's neighbour, whose husband was rarely home. As is usually the case, a kind-hearted soul as it were decided to pass on this information to Reynaud's wife, who wrote immediately to Raoul Dautry. Since our Director took an interest in every aspect of a railwayman's life Reynaud was duly summoned, given a dressing down and taken off the Sables run. No punishment was meted out, since it was not a case of professional misconduct.

Management took his engine and booked him on a 4-6-0 300 Tours service. Without informing me, he asked for me to be transferred with him as fireman. The request was granted, but it didn't really suit me since the new service didn't pay as well. Moreover, I held a bit of a grudge against my direct bosses. They thought that I'd agreed to the shift, even though I hadn't been consulted at all. Still, after all's said and done the new service was a lot more human than the previous one. After a few months my partner's morale, which had suffered after he had been taken off the Sables run, began to perk up.

In 1936, the state rail network began the electrification of the Chartres-Le Mans line. Hence, there was a great need for works trains, especially for installing the catenaries. To bolster the Chartres depot workforce the SNCF called on firemen and drivers from Thouars to help.

Consequently I spent January in the Loupe depot, which was between Chartres and Le Mans. My partner had found a ball of sorts and during the breaks we'd practice bit of rugby – up and unders and passing on the run. One day, when we had parked our works loco on a sideline to let a flock of expresses and goods trains go by and were messing about at rugby, three well-dressed characters appeared. One of them stepped forward and introduced himself.

'I represent *traction* in the trinitarians.'

By trinitarians they meant that they were the three inspectors representing *traction, exploitation* and *voie*. They were rightly feared since they would always arrive unannounced and nothing got past them.

'That's all very well to play a bit of rugby,' said the inspector, 'but have you taken the necessary precautions concerning your parked locomotive? Let's go and have a look.'

The purgers were open, it was in neutral and the tender brakes were on. The water was three quarters up the glass and the pressure gauge at 12 kilos.

'Fine. Good. But the driving wheels haven't been chocked.'

'I haven't got any chocks,' I said, 'anyway there's no chance of her running away.'

'Those are the rules,' he said with a laugh. 'I see you're an old rugby man.'

'That's right.'

'Me too. I played at Toulon. Tight head prop.'

The details were redundant. He must have weighed 100 kilos packed in 1m 80. He'd a vast chest and virtually no neck. If he chanced on the death sentence he'd be tricky to guillotine. We chatted for a while about our common passion, then we shook hands and he left to rejoin his colleagues. The next time I came across him, he was depot inspector during the war.

On 1 February I returned to my home depot and the Tours service along with my partner. The first thing I did at the depot was to report to the *chef de feuille*, who was a young graduate from the Ecole des Arts et Metiers in Paris. He too was a Saintes' man and his father had been an engine driver.

'The boss wants to see you immediately,' he said.

'What's it about?'

'You'll see. Hurry up, he's waiting.'

I went into the *chef de depôt's* office. I'd not had the opportunity to meet him, so he was an unknown quantity. He seemed quiet and introvert and unlike the other chefs, he called you *Monsieur*.

'Monsieur Péroche,' he began and got straight to the point, 'you will be working the 2-8-0 service to Chartres.'

I gaped in disbelief when he told me my driver. The man in question had a terrible reputation (consequently I will not give his name). He had pulled out at the head of the Rochelle-Thouars express half drunk once and he had been in such a bad way that they had to call out a reserve en route. A traction crew had run out in a taxi and brought the train in way behind time.

'I refuse, Sir.' I said. 'I've been assigned by the management to ensure the Tours service and I shall continue to do so.'

'I'm giving you an order. Don't you know I'm in charge here?'

'According to the book, you are not permitted to impose a crewman on me.'

He paused to think a few seconds and calmed down.

'Yes, I know,' he said.' I'll be honest with you about why I chose you for this service. You know the tough sanction that this driver got. He had a reprimand from the Director himself, a last warning and was stood down from touching a steam engine for three months. He should have been dismissed, but somebody further up was looking after him. Perhaps it was a political thing, I don't know. Anyway, I got a note from Paris telling me to put him back on his engine and on his former service and to give him a fireman. That's why you're here.'

'After what you've just said, it's a poisoned chalice that you're offering.'

'Listen Monsieur Péroche, I'm counting on you to take this on.'

I hesitated. I only had to write a letter of refusal, but I had the feeling that it would have been somehow a bad thing to do.

'Very well.'

'You won't regret it. If all goes well to the next maintenance I'll put it in your file and notch you up a place on the drivers' list.'

It wasn't a fool's bargain. Today I can say that it was possibly the best thing I did on the railways.

It was hard leaving my old partner since I both respected and liked him. Some years later he came to a tragic end. He was working the Tours-Thouars express with 4-6-0 300 when he began to have problems. The steam pressure had slipped a kilo and the water wasn't feeding properly. Was it the fireman's fault or was it poor coal? We'll never know. According to the inquiry my friend climbed up on the tender to reach some briquettes on top of the coal and threw down twenty or so to liven up the fire. The fireman refused point blank because the regulations stated that it was forbidden to climb on a moving tender. On professional conscience, my colleague decided to do the job himself. He must have stood up on the tender because his head was taken off as they went under a bridge. Still, show me a fireman who hasn't been up on a moving tender in the interests of the job. I must have done it at least a dozen times.

The day after my interview with the *chef de dépôt* I climbed into the cab of my new engine. I'd met the driver a few times before, but as he was at least 45, or 15 years older than me I addressed him formally using '*vous*'.

'There's no such thing as *vous* on railway engines,' he said. 'We're together for better or for worse so we'd better use *tu*.'

He was a jovial character, an excellent engineer and one of the best driver's I've ever met. If he'd been more serious minded, he could have worked the Pacifics. As it was, he was as cheeky as a court jester.

When we got to Chartres we stopped off for a glass. As we were coming back to the depot for lunch and after our drink he turned to me and said, 'Let's stop a minute in this little café. There's a really pretty waitress I know.'

'No. Let's have our lunch,' I replied firmly.

'You're right,' he said. 'Let's eat.'

We worked together for three months and I managed to help him keep in line. All I had to say was, 'That's enough.'

In return, he always said, 'You're right.'

He knew only too well the road that he'd been down.

The *chef de dépôt* dropped round to see us often when we were with the engine. He shook the driver's hand and then turning to me he'd say, 'I'm pleased with you two. You're

Pacific number 528 arriving at the old Montparansse station at the head of a special (Collection Viollet)

doing an excellent job on the Chartres run. Keep it up. And don't forget Monsieur Péroche, I'm a man of my word.

One May morning we were taking a loco to the Rennes workshops for lifting. We had planned to come back as passengers since we were voting that day in the elections. As it was we were booked to bring back a Pacific to Thouars. We sprinted back without being held up at any stations so that we could get home before the voting stations closed. It was the famous elections in May 1936 that brought the Popular Front to power and brought euphoria to the French – the French working class that is.

With the new government the dream became reality. For the first time in history all working men and women could rest for a few days without losing their pay. Just like all civil servants, the railwaymen already enjoyed paid holidays but these went up from 15 to 21 days a year. At the end of 1936 the 40 hour working week came into force.

The day after the elections the depot chief put me on the Paris-Pacific service. For a while I crewed with different drivers until one day an old Pacific man offered me a permanent place.

'What would you say to working alongside me lad? My engine's a good runner and I've a regular service.'

After a year's wait, I was now well and truly in *Le Grand Service*.

Chapter 4
Le Grand Service

HENRY IV was a legend in his own time. He was a First World War veteran and had been the standard bearer of General Gourand. [1] He sported a blond goatee, had inspiring blue eyes and always wore a sailor's cap.

He looked so much like the famous French king that nobody ever called him by his real name, not even the bosses. He was a fervent patriot and a born engine driver who always put his work before everything. On the other hand, he was very short tempered and flew off the handle for the slightest thing. These minor faults, however, were nothing compared to his immense human qualities.

At that time there were two summer rotas. The first consisted of working the Willotos. These were Pacifics which had been modified to work on low pressure. This meant that they were very versatile. They were also known as call-girls because they didn't have a dedicated driver and the call-boys could ask anyone to drive them. Every day they could have a different team so as to reduce the down time. It was a debatable economy, given the extensive servicing that was necessary at the end of the summer stint.

Henry IV and myself, however, were on the second rota, which consisted of dedicated crews for the Pacifics. It was a crazy service involving around 9,000 kilometres a month. For two ten hour turns we worked the night trains to Paris. These could be goods, cattle or mail trains. These were followed by

---

(1) General Gourand was famous for reporting 'We will stand or die!' when fighting on the Champagne front in the offensive of July 14-18 1918.

the two express services to Bordeaux. Finally we did two ten-hour turns on the Paris-Royan express and then we were back to the night trains to Paris again. Our Pacific 4-6-2 608 was well maintained and she steamed like a dream but was sometimes a little shy on gradients. We made a reasonable living and our careful use of coal meant that we were awarded a traction bonus. This said, the work was hard nevertheless.

I think that the worst thing was starting again after a rest day. We'd book in at midday and then would be on reserve until seven at night. This meant that we had to be ready if there was an engine failure just before departure. We used this waiting time to polish our Pacific. Any crews who failed to keep their locos up to scratch were automatically taken off the *Grand Service* list.

Consequently, with the sun shining down and the engine steamed I used to go over the boiler with a mixture of tallow and wax polish, then I'd shine up the hoops with a special metal polish called *Mirroir*. Needless to say it was hot work and I reckon I lost two or three kilos in sweat alone. Meanwhile Henry IV would look after his connecting rods and valve gear. Of course this was far less arduous, but before becoming a passed driver he'd known the same hardships I had to suffer.

At seven we were relieved by the next reserve crew. As I lived not far from the depot my wife used to come and meet me and we'd go for a drink before going home for the evening meal. At twenty to nine I was back at the depot. In those days we carried our lunch in black straw baskets nicknamed Moses baskets. It had two handles so that you could carry it over your arm and it was big enough to take a litre bottle. This meant we looked like peasants going off to the fields to work. Quite often when walking through the town I'd hear people say, 'There he goes, old black face!'

The electric loco drivers and the guards had leather bags, a far more elegant affair. Needless to say, they were never called black face!

As I walked from the Porte de Paris to the station via the Place Laveau, I'd see folk taking the air or strolling off to the cinema, theatre or perhaps the local bandstand. At times I

Péroche (right)
with Henri IV
(Family
collection)

envied them but I'd always say to myself, 'You chose this job and what's more, you love it.'

On reaching the depot I'd snatch up 24 bricks, each 12 kilos to get the fire going. This was a mixture of full and broken briquettes which I'd lay on the live coals I'd taken from the reserve fire, which was always kept in the depot. The engine gradually got up steam but not enough to blow off the safety valves. If these went off while you were in a station, your traction bonus would suffer. Then it was coupling the engine up to the head of the train which had come from the south west. Next the brakes had to be checked to ensure that the brake pipes on all the coaches were connected properly. At last it was off to Paris. The road was winding as far as the Saumur halt, 30 kilometres out. The safety valves fluttered and sometimes would even blow off, but it was of no account as we were in open country. Between Saumur and Chateau-du-Loir the road became a little hilly but there was no gradient worth mentioning. Then there's a slight incline and as a rule the regulator would be opened up to keep up to regulation speed. This, of course, meant using more water and so the fireman had to stoke the fire more frequently and sometimes even have recourse to the rake. Right after rattling through Sargé-sur-Braye at 90 kilometres an hour we attacked a 10%

gradient some 12 kilometres long. It was essential that the pressure was maintained at this stage and the water level stayed at least half way up the glass. The speed dropped to 50 as the engine slogged up with 550 tons behind. Then Henry IV would coax her speed back up with the maximum steam reaching the pistons and the sparks from the firebox sparkling in the night.

The gradient was on a straight so that on a clear night you could see all the signals well ahead. My partner would take advantage of the situation to take a break. He wouldn't actually go to sleep, but his eyelids would flutter and sometimes his head lolled to one side. Let's just say that he took his mind off the job for a minute or so but still keeping a hand on the sand box lever in case the driving wheels started to slip. There was no chance of me falling asleep, however. I kept an eye on the signals between shovels of coal in the firebox. The water pump was on maximum and I didn't spare the rake.

Once at the summit at Boursay-Saint-Agil, Henry IV cut back the water feed a quarter turn as regular as clockwork. The engine picked up speed and we went back to the small regulator [2] as we ran down through Courtalain and into Bauce.

'Don't you drop off Henry!' I used to say.

The old soldier would give me a sharp look.

'I'm not asleep lad,' he'd answer lifting his head up and pushing his goatee forward.

He'd then take the coffee can, which was kept behind the steam valves to keep it warm, and we'd each have a cup. It was no ordinary coffee however since it was always laced with rum or calva.

At Chartres station a traction crew was waiting to water the tender and bring the coal forward. The water column was opposite the station buffet, so we'd take a quick coffee except when we were on a passenger service, because there were inspectors at every corner and respect for authority is the first step to wisdom!

---

(2) The small regulator is the low pressure regulator used for traveling downhill to economise on steam.

Then it was straight up to Paris. There, the Post Office men took their mail coaches at Montparnasse and we took the rest on to Vaugirard.

After that, we headed for the depot where a worker came to put our fire on stand-by. As a rule I looked after this, but left him to clean out the smoke box. It was usually around half past five in the morning by the time we got to the guard room to wash up. Then it was a cup of well-earned coffee at Bougnate's. At last, after a 21 hour turn, we climbed into bed between the sheets we had brought with us.

After ten o'clock in the morning it was impossible to sleep on account of the whistle blasts and the noise of the compressors. [3] Consequently, we used to get up, slip into our clean overalls, and then we were off for the aperitif. Following a leisurely lunch we took the Montrouge-Montparnasse shuttle service and spent a few hours strolling around Paris. My senator partner was like me, always on the move. Consequently, neither of us had the notion to sleep in the afternoon.

At six in the evening it was back to the depot and back into our work overalls. Henry IV would grease the engine and fuss over his connecting rods, while I got my bricks ready and polished up the copper. While we were having dinner the steam pressure was mounting and after the meal it was back in the cab at the head of what was called the airmail train. It was a very tight run where we had to maintain 120 kilometres an hour up to Chartres. There, our locomotive was uncoupled and replaced by a Mountain Class which took the train to Brittany. At two in the morning we headed a mixed freight and perishables train for Thouars. We were never in the house before eight and the next day we would have to be back on the road to Paris at 10.30 at night.

By comparison, the next two shifts, daytime working on the Paris-Royan train, were pleasant.

Since we had to run at the maximum speed allowed on the track, I'd barely time to give a wave to the women who looked after the level crossings, pretty though they were!

---

(3) Used for pressurising the hot water for cleaning the boilers.

On both up and down journeys there was only one stop at Saumur and since it was impossible to do 300 kilometres with only 22 cubic metres, we had to take water twice while running. This was done using water troughs which were 800 metres long, 40 centimetres wide and between 12 and 15 centimetres deep, which filled up automatically after the passage of each train. One kilometre before the pick up there was a large sign with TROUGH marked on it. This warned the driver to keep his speed down to between 50 and 80 kilometres an hour and remove the pin holding up the scoop. This was a large copper device situated on the tender. As the engine passed the Z sign, which indicated water zone, the two of us would manhandle the lever to lower the scoop into the water trough below. The speed of the train meant that the water was forced up the scoop and into the tender, which filled up in seconds. All that was left to do was to lift the scoop back up and replace the securing pin.

It was on one of these runs that I had the worst experience in my days as a fireman.

It has to be mentioned that there are two types of coal used on the railways. The better of the two is reserved for passenger express trains, while the standard grade is for freight and local trains. The latter is, in fact, a sort of coal dust or screening made up of 60% good and 40% poor quality. It was the same system for briquettes with the better grade known as Aniche or AZ.

One evening, prior to heading the Paris-Royan train from Thouars, we coaled up from the hopper with 6 tons of coal and 2 of bricks ready for the next day. As usual, the steam coal was mixed which meant that some of the larger pieces had to be broken up, but it was all good quality. However, we were flabbergasted to see that the briquettes we'd been issued with were stamped with the word Aigle. This was the cheapest there was.

'We'll have problems with this lot,' I said to my partner.

Henry IV, however, was not one for complaining and he hated altercations with the assistant depot chief.

'Don't you worry lad. The engine steams well and at least

A fine view of a Pacific at Batignolles, Paris, coaled and ready.
Note the size of the tender which carried 23 cubic metres of water
and up to 12 tons of coal. The AZ and ANICHE markings on the bricks
can just be seen
(Collection Viollet)

the coal's good. Your bricks may not be the best in the world but they'll burn.'

This did nothing to stop my worrying, however, because the Royan trains were never easy to fire. The next day, when I was getting the fire up I noticed that the bricks didn't have the same glint as the other grade and they shattered into dust under the hammer rather than breaking into pieces. What's more they burnt with a reddish glow rather than a clear white flame. I felt as if they furnished less calories and I had to open the dampers and use the draught to get enough steam up.

The trouble started after taking on water at Saumur. I didn't spare the rake but the engine wasn't steaming as well as usual and the needle on the steam gauge was struggling to stay on the mark. There were only three centimetres of water in the glass when it should have shown three quarters. I could see quite clearly that old goatee wasn't happy. Moreover, that day it was about 30^0 in the shade and our three litres of water laced with coffee hanging in the breeze on the tender weren't going to be too much. As a rule Henry IV drank one litre and I took the other two.

We steamed through Sargé-sur-Braye on time but with only two centimetres of water to take on the long 10% gradient. My partner opened the dampers a touch but was careful not to upset the engine's cadence. Since I had to keep raking the fire bed, I was sweating like a pig and my goggles were steaming up so much so that I had to take them off. The rubbish in the damned bricks had formed a semi-molten slag which had flowed down through the firebed and solidified when it hit the firebars. Try as I may, there simply wasn't enough air getting to the fire. Would we be forced to stop for water and get the steam back up? Was our prestige train, the pride of the region going to steam in late?

Suddenly I had an idea to unblock the bars. I'd already used the lever to rock the grate but in vain. The slab of slag simply moved with the bars and wouldn't break up. The only thing left was to attack it with the crow bar, which had a chisel end and was actually a tool used by the track maintenance men. I rooted it out from the back of the tender and asked Henry IV to lend a hand. We rammed the bar into the fire with all our strength so as to get a hold of the semi-solid mass. Once we'd pierced it we managed to lift it by using the edge of the firehole as a fulcrum. All through this operation Henry IV kept an eye on the signals, since the stations were flashing by.

The air was getting through at last. The flames got whiter and the needle on the pressure gauge nudged back up. Just after Illiers we picked up our second lot of water from the trough and the level in the glass went up two or three centimetres. Since I'd already downed my two litres of water old goatee gave me what was left of his. But even that wasn't enough to slake my thirst.

We slowed through Chartres. The regulator was three quarters closed, the low pressure gauge showed 1 kilo and the high pressure was between 7 and 8. I opened the dampers full and gave a few strokes of the rake. Coming out of Chartres Henry IV switched to the main regulator to get the engine back up to a 100 kilometres an hour. The low pressure steam was at 3 kilos and the high pressure not far from 15. There were two fingers of water in the glass.

I opened the feed pump more but the needle on the pressure gauge slipped down. The fire simply couldn't manage. I shot a glance at General Gourand's old standard bearer. His blue eyes shone through his goggles but you could see that he was suffering inside. I nodded at the crow bar and we repeated the operation. The heat was so fierce that it singed the hairs on our forearms. When we pulled out the bar it glowed yellow. A few seconds more and it would have melted.

The pressure was back up, but the water had disappeared from the glass. There was nothing left to do but to check on the water using the three safety gauges. [4] I was at the end of my tether. I was so thirsty that I went over to the water tap of the tender. Henry IV grabbed me.

'Don't even think of it!' he said.

I knew full well that the water contained a strong acid to

---

(4) These three valves (*robinets de gauge*) were situated below the glass and used to see what level the water was once it had disappeared from the water gauge. As the water descended so steam would replace the water coming out of the valve or stop cock.

prevent scaling in the boiler but the heat from the fire was overwhelming. I managed to get a hold of myself again and my partner moved back to his post. All this time the ghost train was continuing its road to Paris with all its passengers totally unaware of the footplate drama.

The water wasn't reaching the top valve and only steam came out. Therefore there could only be a couple of centimetres of water covering the crown plate and the fusible plugs. We were now risking everything, it would be a fight to the end. We didn't even look like human beings. Our faces were coal black and only the whites of our eyes and our teeth showed through the blackness. We were just like two devils arguing over the water in the church font which would get us to Paris on time.

We travelled through Trappes at 120 then slowed through Versailles. I took advantage of this to accelerate the water pump. Then we were back up to the line limit. Meudon viaduct came into view, Paris lay before us. The Eiffel tower rose up into a deep blue sky. We rattled through Clamart, Vanves, then Malakoff at 120. The water was now below the middle valve and the bottom one showed a mixture of steam and water. We were at the limit for the plugs.

'Come on lad,' shouted my partner. 'Give the pump and the injectors everything. I want the last drop, dammit. I think we've made it.'

He began to slow the train but kept the regulator wide open to keep what water was left on the crown plate. The regulation speed for entering a station is six kilometres an hour. On that day we came in at fifteen. Better to risk an inspection of the Flamann band than risk the plugs going. Finally we came to rest at the Montmartre buffers. There could only have been a centimetre of water on the crown plate and the gauge showed six kilos of steam but the train was on time and our honour had been saved.

I leapt down from the cab, ignoring the footplate steps, and fell on my Moses basket. Then I began to down a bottle of red like an animal.

'Enough lad!' said Henry, who had followed me down. He

grasped the bottle and finished it off.

The sea of passengers bustled for the exit. They seemed vaguely impressed by the steel beast and gave a furtive glance at the two Negroes who had brought her in safely. I was on the oil chest on the tender with my head in my hands to try to stop the ringing in my ears. I was done in.

'Not a career for the faint-hearted,' I said to myself.

The layman may well wonder why we didn't simply stop at a safety station. The passengers would have only lost 30 or 40 minutes and we wouldn't have risked the catastrophe of the plugs melting. Of course this would have been the logical thing to do and, moreover, it's what our bosses would have advised us to do.

In order to understand our decision I believe you have to be part of the wide family of railwaymen. Henry IV was an elite driver, well loved and respected by his colleagues and trusted by his bosses. It would be impossible to explain how a Pacific like 608 could lose time on a express run. Who would believe a story about being loaded with rubbish bricks? We were seen as a top crew and we had never lost a minute. Henry IV and I were born to win, just like sportsmen and it was a real contest we had on that day both morally and physically. Only one thing counted in the end: we had won.

The shunting foreman signalled us to take the coaches up to Montrouge. But with 6 kilos of steam there wasn't much hope of that. There was little point in telling the truth since he simply would not have believed us.

'The engine's down,' shouted old goatee.

The foreman grumbled irritably. He would have to uncouple the loco and get a replacement to haul out the coaches. At the depot a couple of lads in the yard gave us a hand to break up the clinker and slag with a crow bar. That was the last task of the day.

We went to put our bags and sheets in the guard room and then the bar welcomed us with open arms. We downed a couple of beers and got back to wash up and get our glad rags on.

'Its not sandwiches for us today lad,' said Henry IV. 'After a day like that, we deserve to eat out tonight.'

The down run went better, thanks to 2 tons of Aniche briquettes. Good old 608 steamed like she'd never done before. I reckon she was just trying to make up for the day before.

At the end of August 1936 a breakdown forced us to give up our engine for a couple of days. We were given a replacement 4-6-2, number 775, which was an ordinary loco, with no dedicated crew and so she was absolutely filthy. I didn't have the time to polish her properly because that same evening we were rostered on a cattle train to Paris and then came down, Saturday afternoon with the famous Paris-Royan express. Famous business names often took this train and sometimes MPs who had to be in their constituency on the Sunday. I made do with a quick once over the boiler with a cloth just to get rid of the dirt. She was a powerful engine, steamed well and would have no trouble getting to the City of Light.

The next day I booked into the depot at the usual time but to my astonishment, it was impossible to lay my hands on this locomotive. Despite its being a hundred tons of steel, the engine had simply disappeared. In desperation I spoke to one of the watchmen.

'You don't know where the Thouars 4-6-2-775 is do you?'

'Can't you see her? She's right under your nose.'

Right enough the engine was right in front of my eyes. But I had left her filthy and found her now impeccably clean. The boiler had been scoured the hoops and bearings sparkled and the buffers shone. My eyes jumped out of my head.

The watchman went on, 'You're taking the Director to Thouars. The depot only found out last night. When the assistant depot manager saw the state she was in he decided to give her the works.'

Just at that moment old goatee arrived from the allocation office.

'Have you heard?' he said, 'We're driving the Director. He's opening a velodrome in Thouars.'

As usual Dautry came round to shake our hands before climbing aboard his coach at the front of the train. He went round the engine and congratulated me on her cleanliness. I made sure he knew that I had nothing to do with it.

We reached Thouars without a hitch.

Henry IV shouted to me, 'Come and look at this!'

Between 150 and 200 railwaymen were crowded on the platform blocking the station master's office, the ticket office and the waiting room. Amongst them were shunters and workers from traffic but there wasn't a single fireman among them. As the Director got off the train with his wife and children he was greeted by howls and jeers. It was a real *conduite de Grenoble*.[5] This front line personality, who had come to honour a sports event with his presence was highly annoyed to be treated in such a way in front of his family and a trainload of passengers. He must also have been disappointed after all that he had done for the railwaymen and especially for their children.

In fact the whole thing had been a misunderstanding. The Popular Front had been in power for several months under Leon Blum, whose name should be remembered by the working man, since he had kept all his promises. He'd got them paid holidays, a forty-hour week and collective agreements. Instead of demonstrating to show recognition of this and working harder to help the workers' government, some of them lost their heads and provoked strikes. [6] And so a small group of Thouars railwaymen thought it best to insult Dautry and demand his resignation. To their way of thinking he had no right to be at the head of the nationalised railways.

We found out later that Dautry was in fact a radical

---

(5) In 1832 a costume ball planned by the opposition to King Louis Philippe was cancelled by the prefet. The cancellation caused a riot and the troops charged the crowd, killing 25 people. The troops had to leave the city to the boos of the crowd. The expression Conduite de Grenoble is still used by the French for a difficult or embarassing withdrawal.

(6) These were members of the Communist Party who had refused to join the coalition (see introduction).

Socialist, like his close friend Fernand Chapsal, the senator and mayor of Saintes. Furthermore, after the Liberation, he was to become minister for reconstruction in the left-wing government. The demonstration therefore, had gone for the wrong man and they quickly found out when Dautry agreed to meet their delegation.

But the harm had been done and he would never forgive them for such a public insult. I suspect the delegates remembered for a long time what he said to them on leaving: 'You haven't heard the last of Raoul Dautry.'

The nationalisation of the railways [7] brought about the reorganisation of the lines. Dautry proposed that the Paris-Bordeaux link be changed. The competition between the State line and PO's no longer made any sense. Instead of the usual link through Chartres, Courtalain, Chateau-du-Loire, Montreuil, Parthenay, Niort and Saintes, the trains would go through Poitiers, Niort, La Rochelle, Rochefort and Saintes. The move brought about substantial savings: first, because the Bordeaux, La Rochelle and Rochefort and Saintes trains disappeared and second because the Niort-Saintes link would be covered by diesel multiple units (DMUs), which cost far less to run than steam.

Dautry was from a polytechnic and had a head for figures. The ministry of transport accepted his project, which hasn't been criticised for almost half a century now. But by the same token, the Thouars depot, which was the largest outside Paris became only medium sized. The Pacifics left and a number of fireman and drivers ended up in Le Mans, Montrouge and Nantes after being forced to leave the homes they had built. It was also a severe blow for the shopkeepers in the town too. Some simply reaped what they had sowed but, as always, most of those who suffered were innocent victims.

At that time I was put in the top fifteen in the promotion table to become an apprentice driver. The forty hour week meant that you could move through the ranks more quickly and nominations were slated for 1 January 1937. In October 1936 I was asked if I would accept a posting in one of these three depots: Cholet, La Roche sur Yon or Saint Mariens. I

(7) 1 January 1938 (see introduction).

chose the last. It was a place I knew well and got me nearer to Saintes. Eight days later I was moved to lodgings to await my nomination to apprentice. It was then that I ended my partnership with General Gouraud's standard bearer.

'We were a good team all the same, weren't we Henry IV?'

'Come on lad,' he said, 'never refuse promotion!'

My wife was also sad to leave Thouars, where she had spent some wonderful times. She didn't like the idea of leaving her work as a seamstress, not to mention her friends, but there was nothing that could be done. She left with me to go to Saint-Mariens and found lodgings next to the depot in a terraced of houses belonging to the State railways.

Saint Mariens is a town in the north of the Gironde just on the edge of Charente Maritime. In its heyday it had been an important depot. It had a first class station on the Paris-Bordeax link and was the railhead for Coutras, Libourne, Blaye and Chateauneuf-de-Charente. In the evening at around seven the arrival of the passenger trains from the various branch lines made the place a hive of activity. The buffet had a reputation for fine food, its sweetbread rolls and especially for its famous Blayeau wines. Marshalling all this rolling stock meant that the shunters had to work round the clock. The depot itself was in the municipality of Saint Yzan de Soudiac and employed some 150 workers to maintain its forty locos.

On the 2nd November, the day after taking up my new post I was called to the orders office and handed a letter which I hastened to open – 'Monsieur Peroche has been nominated locomotive driver on grade 8 as from 1 November 1936.' It was a bolt out of the blue. I was running two months ahead of schedule.

After this surprise, I spent several days learning the various roads accompanied by railwaymen who had been nominated at the same time as me. Although I knew the Paris-Bordeaux line I now had to familiarise myself with the links to Coutras, Blaye, Libourne and Chateauneuf. Then came the crucial moment when we were allocated our locos.

At that time, the Saint Mariens depot worked two important services. The 2-4-0 engines were fairly old but ran well and headed the passenger trains. They had 2 metre driving wheels and the firebox was relatively small but they were touchy to drive. The British 2-8-0s headed the goods trains and some passenger services to Bordeuax. These powerful beasts were modern and I'd been familiar with them since my days with driver Launay at the Saintes depot.

I was bowled over when I was allocated a 2-8-0 since it was rare that a locomotive heading a regular service was dedicated to a novice driver. I was to keep this engine for the next two and a half years or just up to the war. As a consequence I was to train up several workmates as firemen and even a driver. These young apprentices always noticed how clean our British engine was and baptised her the 'Golden Loco.'

The only incident of note during this period was in March 1937 at the Saint Andre de Cubzac station. On that night the Gironde was being lashed by a hellish storm. It was pouring down and the wind was unbelievably strong. At three in the morning I was preparing to head up my goods train due to steam out half an hour later. The departure time came and went but I still lacked the square violet signal allowing me to leave. The fire had been banked ready to attack the 10% gradient in the Lormont tunnel and the steam safety valves never stopped chattering. After waiting a fair while I decided to go and look for an explanation. A coach had derailed at the passenger station and prevented us from passing.

At last I got the signal and we managed to make up part of our lost time. At Saint André de Cubzac I stopped for water. My mate got down from the cab and passed me the water hose. Just at that moment, the Bordeaux work train steamed into the station. One hundred and fifty or so people were waiting on the down line platform but the late arrivals couldn't reach it since we were blocking their way.

The station officials appeared and were running about in a tiz. They ordered us to stop taking water. We were to uncouple the train and inch forward so as to leave a space to allow the workers to cross the tracks and reach their train. The whole thing took a good fifteen minutes and of course, meant the workers were going to clock in fifteen minutes late in Bordeaux.

The *chef de gare* was livid.

'You'll pay for these minutes. You shouldn't be taking water anyway!'

'That's a new one!' I replied.

'Take a look at the rule book matey! You were snugged up by the fire, you were! But I can understand that. It's pouring down out here, and we're drenched to the bone. You should have been on the platform with your lamps and loudhailers. Believe me we would have done what we were told.' And on this note we went back to the job in hand under the deluge.

But the affair didn't stop there. Several days later I was asked to fill in a full enquiry form. Saint André station threw everything at me. Loaded with his lies, the station master attacked my conduct while, in reality he had been in bed when the incident occurred. But I was sure I was in the right and I answered that I had stuck to the rules. Three days after, the regional office were at me again with the aim of trying to defend their staff.

Fortunately the *traction* office realised who was really to blame and so asked for an inquiry. That was exactly what I wanted, all the more so since I felt that my bosses would back me up. The enquiry took place eight days later at Saint André in the presence of the *chef d'exploitation,* the *chef de gare* and the *chef de manoeuvres.* The *chef de traction* was represented by an inspector. And then there was the fireman and myself.

I opened the proceedings by asking why the *chef de gare* should be present at all.

'I'm here to defend my staff,' he said.

'Where were you when the goods train arrived?' asked our inspector.

He hesitated for a moment and then decided to admit it.

'I was not yet on duty and was in bed.'

'In that case, Sir, you are not needed here. The inquiry will proceed once you have left the room.'

He left and the meeting started. The two inspectors didn't

pull their punches. The *chef d'exploitation* stood up for his team forcefully but he sensed that he didn't have a case. Our man was merciless and gave me a wink of encouragement. I defended myself indignantly because in cases like this better to be the butcher than the bull.

After an hour a decision was taken and the report signed. The *traction* section was freed of all responsibility for the incident and the whole affair was blamed on *exploitation*.

I heard later that the *chef de gare* received a written reprimand (which went in his file) while the station assistants were only reprimanded.

Every week we worked the same train and sometimes it took us an hour to take water. For a month not a word passed between us and they watched us like hawks. But time is a great healer. The episode was gradually forgotten and we became bosom friends. A fine bottle used to wait for us when we made the halt, which all goes to show that the association of railwaymen is like one big family. There can be professional, union or political arguments but the job itself is the cement of firm friendship. This love of your work is the same for sailors, miners and all pursuits that entail toiling in hard conditions.

In February '38 we were asked where would prefer to be posted if we were nominated. Anywhere, was my answer of course. In any case I didn't expect to become a passed driver so soon, but at the end of the month, on the down trip from Chateauneuf sur Charente, I came across a friend of mine in Barbézieux station.

'The nominations are in at Saint-Mariens,' he shouted. 'We've been promoted, both of us.'

I couldn't believe it, but when I got to the depot the proof was there. I stopped by the office to sign for my nomination and then got ready to celebrate the occasion with a good few drinks.

And so I became a passed driver at thirty years old, only three years after becoming a passed fireman. From now on I'd be treated differently and travel in second class! [8] I'd reached

---

(8) There were three classes at that time.

my goal. I must admit that the *Front Populaire* and the forty hour week had a lot to do with this rapid promotion. As good luck often comes in twos, my little girl was born in Saintes on 14 July.

And yet my little Madeleine nearly became an early orphan. In fact it was on Christmas day 1938. I was rostered on a passenger train in the morning and was to leave after, at nine at night, with a freight train to Saintes.

In the afternoon my wife would go to my parents' with my little daughter ready for the party later at night. My train was due in Saintes around midnight and I was to meet up with my family at around one in the morning.

I left Bordeaux on time and was soon slogging up the 1 in 10 gradient through the Lormont tunnel. We were making 45 kilometres an hour, which wasn't bad considering there was 860 tons behind. I regularly gave a touch of sand because water seeping through the roof made the rails very wet. Suddenly, around 400 metres into the tunnel the whole train stopped in its tracks. Luckily we were only doing around 20 kilometres an hour at the time. I shot a glance at the air pressure gauge: the needle was at three instead of the usual five kilos yet the main reservoir showed eight – which was normal. A connecting air pipe had probably come loose and so triggered the automatic brake. I'd have to inspect the train and repair the broken connection.

Just as in the good old days of the ancient Gauls, we had but torches to illuminate our way when we were outside the engine. In fact it was simply a copper pipe, with some wool soaked in paraffin crimped at one end. This gave of a red light and black smoke. I lit up my torch but it went out almost immediately because the carbon dioxide and the smoke coming from the loco put paid to any combustion through lack of oxygen. Why couldn't this mishap have taken place 400 metres up the line in the open air?

I took my pocket electric lamp and got down to look for a spare connecting hose and a spanner from the tender. My feet had no sooner touched the ground than I was on my knees almost choking from the thick sulphurous smoke coming from the engine. For a second I thought my time had come. My lungs were struggling, but in vain. It looked as if I would die of suffocation in this God-forsaken tunnel – killed by my own locomotive!

Luckily I managed to get my breath back by staying close to the ground where there was a slight current of air coming from the north end of the tunnel. I took deep breaths, got myself together again and made my way to the tender. There I grabbed a spare connecting hose, a spanner, a hammer and a cold chisel. I headed south, down the train. The further I got from the loco, the easier it was to breathe.

I checked fifty or so wagons one by one but without finding the damaged hose. Then, on the last few I found the guilty party. It was the last but one.

While I was doing this, the guard had left to place two warning flares 200 metres from the rear of the train and a further two at 800 metres because if halted in a tunnel the safety measures were doubled. Once I'd replaced the hose I tightened the joints at both ends. As soon as I'd done this the airflow was restored and all the brakes released. However, since we were on a 1 in 10 grade the 860 tons of freight plus the 130 tons of engine meant that the train started to go back.

Normally, when this happened, the fireman put the brakes on. But the train still rolled back. I had a horrible thought – had my mate noticed that the train was moving? Had something happened to him? Was he checking his fire? Yet again I thought my time was up. Miraculously I managed to get myself together and clamber onto the rear buffers. I was safe – but the train was still rolling back and I got myself ready to disconnect the air hose to stop the train automatically again. At last, however, the fireman activated the air brake and the heavy string of wagons came to a halt.

The old guard came back panting and wheezing after his two kilometre run (he was no Olympic champion!). Once he was back in the guard's van I made my way back to the cab. Although the engine was still smoking hellishly the carbon dioxide had cleared a little.

We still had to start the train on a gradient with our 860 tons behind. The fire was healthy and the safety valves fluttered showing that the pressure was there. I let the engine and tender brakes off and waited for the slight pull backwards. The engine and tender buffer springs compressed as the engine inched back onto the stationary wagons. I opened the regulator and the superheated steam arrived at the distributor and then the piston heads. Nothing moved for a few seconds but the steam increased and the train nudged forward. The 400 metres to the end of the tunnel seemed to take an eternity. Then the engine burst into fresh air. We were under an incredible starry sky. It was like heaven itself.

I got into Saint Mariens an hour late and headed off for the capital of the Saintonge after taking water. When we pulled into Saintes station the bells were ringing for the end of midnight mass. I left the depot and walked up to Saint Eutrope, the very place where I was born. I arrived at my parents but there wasn't a light to be seen. It was gone two o' clock and they'd decided not to wait any longer. I ate what they'd left me with a heavy heart as I pondered on how I may have ended my days in the tunnel. I went up to see my wife who had stayed awake with worry.

'What happened?'

'I'll tell you later.'

It took me a while to get to sleep. I believe that I'll remember the Christmas night of '38 for the rest of my days.

In 1939 the Saint Mariens depot saw some big changes since the network office disappeared and was replaced by the SNCF which radically changed all the existing structures. A lot of passenger trains were replaced by DMUs and some branch lines by coaches. The reason was that all these were said to be more economic than steam. Steam trains were only used for freight and work trains to Bordeaux.

There were now too many train crews and passed fireman and drivers were asked what depots they'd be prepared to accept. Those who put Niort and Rochelle were transferred quickly. As for me, I hoped it might be a chance to go back to my hometown, but on the first of August 1939 Germany invaded Poland. It wasn't a good time to make plans.

Péroche (right) with
crew members and
a local anxious to
be in the picture.
The locomotive is
the German
Mountain Class
mentioned in the
text
(Family collection)

Chapter 5
The Taurus Orient Express

THE EARLY DAYS of September 1939 called for exceptional demands and the railways were mobilised in record time. It was a complete success and the SNCF and the railwaymen were cited for the Order of the Nation.

Saint Mariens became the leading depot for the Saintes region and was bolstered by a large number of skilled men. Top-line drivers and repair men arrived, not to mention additional administration staff and even retired train crews. These retired men had left the service at fifty, but for five years were liable for mobilisation for hauling trains. The depot also received a considerable quantity of new material. There was around twenty 4-6-0 800s and even 2-4-0s which were used to head up passenger trains. Last of all, a 50 ton crane arrived at Saintes.

This wave of new staff caused an accommodation problem because Saintes was a small place. The few hotels there were, along with the lodgings at the station itself, were reserved for the bosses. As for the rest, we pitched some tents in the grounds next to the depot. The beautiful autumn weather was ideal for camping. Those of our workmates who didn't have particular skills were enlisted in their respective regiments.

My brother, however, who was an engine driver based in Paris, did his service in the Engineers and was taken prisoner in 1940.

For three weeks or so we worked like devils. There wasn't any question now of working to the rulebook, the forty hour week or even taking rest days. We were working shifts of twelve to fourteen hours without a break. Sometimes we'd be back on shift after only a couple of hours sleep. Our role was to get the troops to the front line in the shortest time possible. I was very young in 1914 but I can remember clearly the soldiers leaving and all shouting 'To Berlin!' with the flowers in their rifle barrels. How different it was in 1939! The men were grim and had a sombre air about them. You could see that they were sad to leave their wives and children.

It was not long after war was declared that a *traction* inspector arrived at the depot to take on the job of *chef de dépôt*. We all recognised him at once. He was the giant from Toulouse who had given me a rigorous inspection when I had been playing rugby next to a site where they had been carrying out electrification on the line. In no time at all we were talking about our favourite sport.

He liked the good things in life and had all the good points of the folk from the Midi: openhearted, expansive, a straight-faced joker, he was always winding up his men. He loved good food and was a great drinker of Pernod and Ricard.

'I'll spend as I earn, but I'm not going to lose an ounce,' he proclaimed. At midday and at six he'd turn to his sergeant major and say, 'Right then lads let's get a move on it's time for a Pernod.' He was really afraid that these delightful spirits would disappear because of the war. Fortunately his powers of foresight enabled him to take adequate and timely precautions. Contrary to popular opinion this amazing man said right from the start that the war would be a long one.

'It'll take a long time to use up all the weapons in the world today,' he said. 'This war will last four or even five years, mark my words.'

As a result he called on the owner of the small café just next to the depot. He asked her to change the inventory concerning her stock of aperitifs. Then, with her agreement, he commandeered a couple of track men to dig a hole in her neighbour's garden. There, they buried around 150 bottles of Pernod, Ricard and de Berger. The other bottles held no interest for him. Thanks to his foresight the traction staff had exclusive rights to these fine spirits throughout the entire war. He'd often invite his officers for a glass. 'Here you are,' he'd announce, 'this isn't your ersatz rubbish, it's the real pre-war stuff.'

He was also one for the black market. I was coming home once with the 5922 from Bordeaux and just before Saint-Mariens I ran over several detonators. I slowed down to walking speed in line with the regulations. Then just coming round a curve, where visibility was short, I saw a red flag and two more detonators on the track. This meant come to a complete stop. I respected the command scrupulously. The inspector and the *chef mécanicien* appeared out of a thicket. These safety tests took place quite often and the inspector showed no mercy for any offenders. Anyone trying to bend the rules would get a reprimand and could say good-bye to his year-end bonus.

'That's good Péroche,' he said.' Now get a move on and we'll see you at six.'

'And what about that?' I said, nodding at two bunches of asparagus which he had under his arm and which he'd obviously bought at a local farm.

'None of your business,' he answered.

An hour later my mate and I were around the table with the inspector and the head driver. We had three or four rounds and I had all the time in the world to size up the Toulonais. He downed his drinks seriously with his eyes raised to heaven as if to thank the good Lord for the privilege of savouring the beverage. With such a diet, it wasn't long before he was up there to thank him personally. It was before he even retired if my memory serves me well.

After the mobilisation of French troops, the demand for trains eased up and our bosses took advantage of this to give us some rest. Soon it was dead calm since the economy was turning slowly and freight movement was limited. The train crews who had been called up out of retirement remained on duty for one more month following a decision by the War Ministry. At that time I was working with a 55 year old driver who must have weighed 130 kilos or so. Of course this meant I went back to being fireman. Soon, however, the old timers were sent home and the engines given back to their dedicated crews. Then it was winter, and a hard one it was too. In December the Saintes' *chef de bureau* made an inspection of Saint-Mariens. I knew him well since I'd been under him in my days at Thouars.

'Péroche,' he said to me, 'I'd like to see you. I've got something confidential to tell you. There's talk of raising a company of railwaymen for a posting in the Middle East. Syria to be precise.'

He looked at me without saying anything further. Why was he telling me all this?

'The army's asking for young, fit men,' he went on. 'Along with the *chef d'arrondissement* we've drawn up a list of likely candidates. In theory it's two men per depot. I've put your name forward for Saint-Mariens.'

'Thank you Sir, but it's a poisoned chalice if you ask me.'

'That's as maybe. Anyway nothing's been decided yet. It all depends on how the war turns out.'

The conversation was left there and as time went by I felt that the project had been dropped. My conclusions however were a little too hasty. At the end of February I was sent for, along with one of the depot's firemen, to see the boss. He was standing by his desk, note in hand, when we entered. His face was pale and his look sombre.

'Well my lads, you're off to war.'

'Not in the ranks I hope,' I said derisively, since I wasn't surprised by the news.

'Look here Péroche, be serious for once. Report at Orleans tomorrow at 1700 hours. You'll be in cavalry uniform and then you'll be taken to your destination, as yet unknown.'

The note contained nothing more but I was fairly sure where we were to be posted.

'We're off to Syria,' I said to my mate. 'That's official. I know. Believe me we won't be in the cavalry but the 8th Railway Division.'

I spent my last few hours of freedom saying farewells to

my friends and family then I made my way to Bordeaux with
the fireman to catch the Paris-Hendaye train. At 1600 we were
in Aubrais station. A corporal gathered up all the arrivals and
shipped them out to the cavalry barracks.

The next morning we were decked out imperially. The
uniforms were brand new and clearly just out of the factory. I
was perplexed when I was issued with an officer's uniform and
was even more surprised to see the three stripes sewn on the
cuffs. Why should a railwayman second class be suddenly
promoted to a sergeant? Was it a case of mistaken identity? I
soon found the key to the mystery. The military railwaymen
posted in the railway regiment took the grade corresponding
to their qualification. The track men and workers were
ordinary soldiers, the firemen were brigadiers (like my mate
from Saint Mariens) and by the same token our captain was
the Marseilles *chef de dépôt*. For the first time in my life I
sported stripes on my arm that I'd never earned. That evening
the soldiers kept saluting me in the streets of Orleans. That
really took the biscuit.

We left the next day for our mystery destination. The word
Syria had not even been mentioned. Some men talked of
North Africa, but I still held on to what my boss had told me
in Saintes. We travelled down to Toulouse, where we took the
Bordeaux-Marseilles train. From the station we were taken by
military trucks to the Saint Marthe barracks, where I'd been
thirteen years before for a few days before leaving for Algeria.

After a wait of several days we boarded a handsome steam
ship called the *Patria*. There weren't many soldiers but there
were a lot of Jewish passengers who had been expelled from all
over the place, who were making their way to Judea since the
state of Israel hadn't yet been created.

Our captain was hoping that all the 178 members of the
section could mess together in one of the three sittings,
because in the railway service every one has the same rank. But
we had forgotten we were now in the army. The rules were
strict and couldn't be bent. The troopers, brigadiers and
corporals would eat in the hold along with the horses. The
warrant officers would take the first sitting with the second
class passengers while the officers sat in the third sitting along

with the more important passengers in first class. The second sitting was reserved for warrant officers and the wives of the career officers and soldiers serving in the Lebanon and Syria.

Our lieutenant told me and a driver from Cherbourg to see the dining room manager. We were to try and get all our officers to eat together. On meeting the head of the dining room I had the impression that I'd seen him before.

'I do believe I know you,' I said. 'We've already met; but where?'

'I had the same feeling when I saw you,' he replied. 'You're one of the railwaymen aren't you? I served more than ten years in the restaurant cars you know.'

'But France is a big place.'

'I was on the Nantes-Bordeaux line.'

'I'm from the Saint Mariens depot.'

'I don't believe it! The famous sweetbread rolls of Saint Mariens! What's become of Ferdinand? and Andréa?'

'They're still working in the buffet. That's where we must have met!'

We became bosom friends from that moment on.

'I'll put you both down for the second sitting. It's at midday – the best time really – and you'll be surrounded by pretty girls, what's more! I make the decisions here you know,' he finished proudly.

My friend from Saint Mariens was of a delicate constitution and the very idea of eating in the hold alongside the horses had shattered him.

'It'll be revolting,' he'd told me, completely dispirited. 'We'd be eating from mess tins like common soldiers while you'd be in the dining room with your Bordeaux wines, hors d'oeuvres juicy meals, desserts, cakes and coffee!'

'I know, I know!' I said. 'It's bad luck. There's no rank in an engine cab but the army's the army. I'll talk to the dining room boss. If anything can be done he's the one to do it.'

Consequently, just before the first service I invited my old dining-car friend for a glass and asked him about my friend.

'Impossible,' he said, 'if they checked up I wouldn't hear the end of it.'

He thought for a while and then said, 'It may be all right in fact. There's a free seat not far from you. Listen, he'll have to get a warrant officer's jacket.'

Nothing could be easier than borrowing a jacket from one of his officer friends on the first sitting. And so it was, for the entire voyage, my friend ate with the warrant officers.

The crossing began like a real pleasure cruise. On the very first day while I was watching the 8th regiment come aboard I noticed a very pretty blonde girl. When she passed by me I gave her a look. In return she nodded her head and said, 'Good day captain.'

She'd taken my three diagonal stripes to be the three horizontal stripes of a captain. She came up to me, held out her hand and introduced herself. She was an English woman from London. I was more than a bit fluffed by her mistake and so I simply introduced myself by name without mentioning my rank.

'Look at those smart lads coming aboard,' I said pointing to my friends decked out in spanking new uniforms.

'Some of them look quite old,' she said.

It was true that some of the volunteers were well over forty.

'They don't look very warlike,' she went on.

'Their looks are nothing to go by. When the enemy's in front of them they'll fight like lions.'

On the following days she'd often ask me to take the aperitif with her. We'd have a whisky and I had to insist on paying. As she spoke French fairly well we chatted about one thing and another. I discovered that her parents in London were wealthy and she was on her way to Haifa to see her brother who was a career officer.

One day I had the strong impression that she was sulking and at last she explained why.

'You're not a captain at all.'

'That's true. But then I never said that I was. It was you that gave me the rank. What would you have done in my place?'

I see she said breaking into a laugh. 'When I found out I wasn't pleased at all, but now I forgive you. You're a nice man all the same even though you're not a captain. Anyway *chef* let's have a whisky.'

We pressed on towards our destination. After following the Corsican coast to the straits of Bonifacio, we saw the impressive sight of Stromboli with its glowing eruptions at night. Next it was the straits of Messina between Sicily and Italy with Reggio in the distance and Etna smoking. The weather was beautiful up to Good Friday, then a storm blew up as we approached Crete. Violent gusts of wind swept over the Mediterranean and enormous waves made the ship heel over, with a number of passengers suffering from sea sickness. Fortunately it was fine again the next day.

Despite everything, no one could forget that we were at war.

German submarines had been sighted in the Mediterranean and we would have been torpedoed had we been spotted. At night the *Patria* sailed on with all lights out and no smoking on deck. Some passengers went as far as to sleep on deck with their life jackets on.

We reached Haifa on Easter day. The commissioned and warrant officers received permission to go ashore while the ordinary soldiers remained, in company with the horses. Once on land I sensed I was in the East with its strong fragrances and sparkling colours and brightly dressed crowds. English soldiers and sailors have memories of the West, but for the French, it's always been the East.

We weighed anchor around nine in the evening to enter the beautiful port of Beirut at five the next morning. It was an incredible sight. Behind the town, which reminded me of

Algiers, there rose a chain of majestic mountains capped with snow. The sun came up and gilded the peaks with purple. It was still early April but it was already warm and the street traders were offering cherries for sale to passers by.

The weather was perfect for the disembarkation and the army trucks then took us to the T2 camp situated to the east of the town in the foothills of the mountains. There we stayed for a fortnight with nothing to do except take walks, eat in the town and visit the Place des Canons where you can see the most beautiful girls in the world.

I had an advance of a staff sergeant and so I was fairly affluent. My wife received my fixed wage, a lodging allowance and half my traction bonus. Consequently I had the satisfaction of knowing she was being looked after financially. As for being looked after emotionally, that was a different story. But given the dramatic state France was in, she wasn't the only one to suffer.

All the other military staff in Beirut had been issued with cotton uniforms while we were still sweating in our woollens. No one really knew what to do with us – even our officers. It was obvious we weren't there to drive the rack railway or the narrow gauge Beirut service. Some mentioned Aleppo, which was the most important railhead in Syria, which was on the Orient express route.

One fine day we learnt that we were to be reviewed by the High Commissioner for the Lebanon, General Weygrand. The news put our officers in a flap. They feared this famous general who had the reputation of being a stickler for discipline and the military code.

'He's a tough one apparently. We're going to look real amateurs,' we said.

They made us fall in, stand to attention, at ease, then march in step. But as they were all railwaymen they knew no more than we did about military matters. They had a hard time getting us to march in step but on seeing the result they couldn't stop themselves laughing.

'Come on now lads, let's be serious and make an effort.'

Fortunately the review went better than expected. Weygrand arrived in full dress uniform with leggings.

'Attention!'

Everybody froze to attention and remained absolutely still. He looked us over, one after the other. The heat was stifling.

'At ease!'

Weygrand knew he was dealing with railwaymen and was lenient. He then explained what awaited us.

'You are to be posted to Aleppo. A second front is planned for the Balkans and Turkey will fight with the Allies. [1] There are only two main railways in the Near East. The first is the route of the Orient Express, which comes in from Turkey and crosses the Syrian frontier at Medein (Mardin). It then passes through Aleppo before crossing the Euphrates and on to Mosul and Baghdad. The second goes from Aleppo to Rayaq. To reinforce the second front we need more logistics and railwaymen. Hence the creation of the 8th railway division. Last, there are fifty-five German locomotives, which are at this moment to be found in Eastern France and they will make their way to Aleppo via the Simplon, Orient Express line. As you can see, everything has been taken care of.'

He then went on to say what he expected of us.

'As well as the hostilities you will also have to cope with the climate. Your fellow countrymen are doing their duty on the French front. You will do yours here, but conditions will perhaps be worse. Above all beware of alcohol. I recommend you to add arak to the water and not vice-versa. I put my trust in you gentlemen.'

A few days later at around ten in the morning we set off for Rayaq on the rack railway. I was expecting to see an old rattletrap like the little economy trains of bygone days. You can imagine my surprise when I saw the line. The engine had 400

---

(1) The Nazi-Soviet non-aggression pact of August 1939 prompted Turkey to sign a treaty of mutual assistance with Britain and France in October. Hedging its bets, the government concluded a non-aggression treaty with Nazi Germany on June 18, 1941, just four days before the Axis invasion of the Soviet Union.

tons to haul up gradients of one in six or seven. The fireman stoked his furnace and the driver put the last drops of oil on the bearings. Both of them were bathed in sweat.

The loco was equipped with modern fittings. Amongst these were two sets of high-pressure cylinders. The first was on the outside just like an ordinary single expansion type and the second was inside under the boiler. When the profile of the track meant that the first set couldn't haul the train, the driver engaged the second set on the rack. The power was doubled and the driver had two engines to get him up these very steep grades. Consequently, the train slowly climbed up more than 2,000 metres, just like a silk worm crawling up a mulberry branch!

As we climbed the town of Beirut slipped into the distance until it was just like a small nest in the vastness of Lebanon next to the bright blue of the Mediterranean Sea. At seven in the evening, at the summit of a pass, we were in Syria. There was snow on the ground and icicles hung from the rocks. The thermometer had gone from 28^0 to -3^0 or -4^0. Despite the powerful heating we were glad of our woollen uniforms.

We arrived at Rayaq at night and then took the ordinary train on to Aleppo. At around eleven in the morning we pulled into a vast, incredibly beautiful, modern station.

The *souks* of the old town are not as famous as those in Tunis but they are much bigger – sometime several kilometres long. The French soldiers were strongly advised not to frequent these markets as they were deemed dangerous. The modern town is just the opposite. It's criss-crossed with splendid avenues and lined with fine buildings. At first sight the most striking aspect of the town was the total absence of automobiles although the petrol from the oil well at Mosuk was almost cheaper than water. However, main roads were rare and the standard of living quite low. For the French arriving in Aleppo everything seemed cheap. Cars were only for teachers, doctors, French army officers and some potentates.

Motorised taxis didn't exist and you had to make do with carriages called *arrabadjis*, which were pulled by one or two scrawny horses which appeared to be barely alive. When I was going to book in at the depot I'd always take a two horse taxi so that if one collapsed en route there was always the other one to get me there in time for my train!

The 8th Railway Brigade wasn't like the other brigades. Instead of barracks we stayed in a disused hotel and we were allowed complete independence. We had a large kitchen, a dining hall and bedrooms fitted with decent beds.

'Look at those railwaymen', we'd often hear said, 'always with their privileges'.

Two days after we moved into the hotel our bosses took us to see the loco sheds which were just next to the station. We were surprised to see how modern they were with the engines in good shape and clean as a whistle. The local managers were pleasant and the Syrian *chef de dépôt* was an engineer who had studied in a French Civil Engineering School.

There too, we were given the run of the place. Our officers assumed the roles of *chef de feuille*, *chef mécanicien* and *chef des réparations*. But first of all we had to know which of the lines we were to run. The links Aleppo-Rayaq and Aleppo-Mosulk were those we expected. I was asked to check over a line but without saying if I was to go as far as Rayaq or even if I was to make a halt on the run.

My mate fell ill just before we were due to leave on and I found myself alone on the evening express with a few tins of food and a litre of Algerian wine. I showed my authorisation to the Syrian driver, who, like his fireman barely spoke a word of French. Both of them were as thin as the horses that pulled the *arribadjis*, but both knew their jobs and the engine itself was exceptionally clean.

Soon we were rolling through the Syrian countryside but without saying a word to each other. As night fell I didn't feel too happy. The presence of my partner would have cheered things up. The two Syrians climbed down in the station for a few moments to get some food and began to eat while looking after the engine. The fireman took mouthfuls between strokes of shoveling coal and the driver chewed away as he leaned out of the cab to check the signals. I was stupefied to see what these men had to eat: a peeled cucumber with no oil nor vinegar, two raw tomatoes, some chicory and a few maize biscuits. It's true that in these hot countries, meat, sauces and charcuterie aren't recommended. As a matter of fact, however, these people are rarely ill despite working extremely hard.

At around one in the morning the train pulled into Hims station. I got down from the engine and without saying a word made my way through the passenger exit. The whole exercise of learning the road had been a waste of time since I'd seen nothing during the whole trip. I had a terrible thirst and could have done with something to eat. Although it was late, the town was lit up and the streets were crowded. In these countries there's not a cat on the streets between one and five in the afternoon, but the people go to bed very late.

I stopped in front of a well-lit, handsome building with an illuminated sign in Arabic. As I was in clean overalls and my face wasn't too dirty I decided to pay a visit. There was music and a good few clients. Some of these were drinking and others smoking hookahs amongst some really beautiful, almost naked, girls. I thought twice about sitting down in this night club but my thirst decided for me. Since I was the only European, several heads turned and stared at this strange looking creature.

Two girls pitched up and sat down, one on each knee. The sharks were out. They didn't speak a word of French and it cost me a drink apiece to get rid of them. I downed a beer in one and beat a hasty retreat from the den of iniquity, making my way back to the station to await the 4 a.m. express.

The next day my boss asked what I had learnt.

'Didn't see a thing,' I stated.

'That's no matter. We won't be running that line anyway. 'Four hundred kilometres in heat like that, it's out of the question. There's none of you would make it back to France. In fact, we're allocating you a stretch of the Orient Express road which goes from Aleppo to the Turkish border. It's about 80 kilometres. We'll be looking after all the trains – passenger and freight alike.'

Consequently I left with my partner to learn the road as far as Meidan-Ekbes. When we climbed into the cab of the Taurus Orient Express at ten in the morning the heat was already overwhelming. The Syrian climate is even worse than that of North Africa. I witnessed temperatures of 43^0 and even 45^0 in the shade. In summer it's usually between 35^0 and 40^0 in the daytime. Running steam trains in temperatures like these was something terrible. But that's what we were there for.

It's impossible to compare the French countryside with these desert landscapes. In France, learning the road is helped by numerous reference points: villages, farms, woods or copses for example. In this God-forsaken place we sometimes ran 12 or 15 kilometres without seeing a tree or a house. We'd often see vultures tearing away at a dead camel. In these burning red lands the desolation is only broken by water holes which support sparse vegetation. Only at the rare oases are there any towns such as Mouslimiyé Ama and Radjou.

The train arrived at Meidan at two in the afternoon. It was a small town of 2,000 people and was situated on the Turkish border on the banks of the river Karasu.

On the opposite side of the river we could make out the Turkish guard posts with the red flag and the star and crescent. The Syrian loco was uncoupled and stabled in a small engine shed. A Syrian railwayman started up a steam engine to pump up water from the depths to replenish the tender.

We ate at the buffet of the international station where the owner spoke French. We didn't have to eat there since we had been issued with tinned food and bread but the menu looked tempting. There were cucumber, tomato and onion salads with peppers, chicken spiced with herbs, wild rabbit and partridge and quail.

The mayor, or the *mouktar* as he was called, came over to see us. He was squat and looked around 40. He wore a shirt and shorts.

'You are the very first railwaymen to visit my town,' he said in perfect French. 'I've heard that you'll be looking after the line and that sometimes you'll be lodging in the town. I hope your stay will be enjoyable. Syria is not as beautiful as France, a country I know well, but we will try to make the separation from your homeland as bearable as possible.'

He showed us round the town hall, the public gardens in full bloom and then we visited the village school. As we went in the teacher told all the children to stand up and they gave us a perfect rendering of the Marseillaise.

'You see,' said the mouktar, 'even though we are Syrians first, we also think of France.'

We were very touched by this gesture of our homeland. You always love your mother country more when you are far away from her.

Around five in the afternoon he invited us to his home and offered us cakes, cream cakes and small maize rolls. It was a splendid meal washed down with arak and even some beers and bottles of fine Bordeaux. The *mouktar* appeared to be a true democrat and he spoke of France with admiration. He added, all the same, that news of the war so far made him worried.

'You must invite your captain,' he said as he left us.

During our first night on the Turkish border the mosquitos prevented us from getting a wink of sleep. We'd been issued with mosquito nets but they had more holes in them than a gruyere cheese. In desperation we got up and walked down by the river. Opposite us lay Turkey under a clear sky, bright with stars. We gazed up at the North star, the Great Bear and the Little Bear which twinkled in the eastern sky and my thoughts were back in France. Four and a half thousand kilometres away people were gazing at the same stars with, perhaps, even the same thoughts. But soon the cold got the better of us. In these countries the temperature varies as much as thirty degrees, between midday and three in the morning. It was because of this our lieutenant major had ordered us to wear a sort of woollen sash at night.

After having checked the Aleppo-Meidan route two or three times I submitted a written certificate that I had sufficient knowledge of the road. Some 40 locos had arrived from France and the men of the 8th brigade had got them in working order. They were going to head all the trains with no exception since the DHP, the Syrian Rail Company, had abandoned this branch entirely. For the three Taurus-Orient expresses a week, the company allocated us two German Mountain locomotives. These were 901 and 902 equipped with ten driving wheels. We were situated in the foothills of the Turkish mountain chain and we would have to cope with 25% gradients. Some might be surprised that Germany had continued to supply railway equipment to Syria, which had been under French mandate since the Treaty of Versailles in 1918. Syria, however, just like the Lebanon had originally been Turkish Asia and had fought alongside the axis powers in the First World War. Consequently the Germanic roots were still alive. These were also seen in the signalling system and the style of uniform. When we climbed down from the engine at stations the people would stare at our blue overalls curiously and so the prestige of being a railwayman and our pride in France took a knock – but it was nothing serious. While they were there the Germans could have rectified the really weak point of the Syrian rail network and that was the track. This was not laid out efficiently and the foundation was weak because of a lack of ballast and good oak sleepers. The engines heeled over more than in France and they couldn't be expected to perform as well as at home.

At last we were ready to start. To be honest, the volunteers didn't queue up to crew trains when it was 40^0 in the shade. Certain absences were justified, but a lot of the men feigned sickness to avoid these inhuman conditions. This was probably why no-one volunteered to take my place when I was assigned to the Orient express. The rules stated that this famous international express could only be allocated to drivers authorised to head fast trains and expresses but although I hadn't actually been to the finishing school at Le Mans I was on the list. The *chef de feuille* was from Saint Jean station in Bordeaux and hardly knew me at all, nevertheless he took to me and showed his trust by incorporating me into the express service. When it was pointed out to him that I didn't have the qualifications of a senator he simply answered, 'He's my responsibility.'

So that was that, and for three months I had the joy of heading these trains – and without the slightest mishap. There were six drivers from the southeast and three from the Western Region in charge of the trains to Meidan. My other two regional colleagues came from La Rochelle and Cherbourg.

The firemen had to be hardy since they really had their work cut out. Fortunately men from the depot helped them out by turning the engines round and cleaning out the firebox. In turn, the drivers gave them a hand by helping to bring the coal forward from the tender. My crew mate was from Saint Mariens. He was an excellent fireman but not built for the job. He managed the first shift with me but in the second showed that he didn't have the stamina for these superhuman tasks. He simply couldn't top the return trip and had to come back to Aleppo as a passenger. He was temporarily replaced by a 30 year old Syrian depot foreman. He did his utmost but after the eight hour run he arrived at Aleppo totally exhausted.

As a permanent replacement I was given a driver from Le Mans, whose sister was married to a Saint Mariens foreman. He was a stout lad in perfect health and stood up well to the heat. He stayed with me until the end of June, that is until the Armistice was signed.

If I had to sum up this time in one word it would be thirst. In order to cope with the intense heat from a steam-engine's firebox working under a blazing sun we had to consume vast quantities of liquids. All those who accused us of exaggeration showed only their ignorance. This was just the sad case with an admin lieutenant.

One evening we were having dinner in the guard room when a lieutenant from the order office came up to me.

'I say Péroche, is it you that drives the Orient Express?'

'That's right.'

'Well Sir, I'm travelling with you on the engine tomorrow. I've got written authorisation from the captain.'

This decision took me aback since it was madness to travel in the cab when you could travel in ideal conditions in the coaches. Still, I reckoned it was best not to ask questions.

The next morning the lieutenant joined us on engine 901 while we were getting her ready. I hardly recognised him since he had swapped his military uniform for blue overalls and a Basque beret. He explained right away his reasons for joining us. The previous day the *chef mécanicien* had returned from the Turkish frontier full of complaints. He said to any that would listen that it was inhuman to drive steam trains in such a heat.

'Well Sir, after all, it is your job,' the lieutenant had commented. To which the *chef* suggested, 'I'd like to see you do it. I bet you wouldn't go the full trip on the footplate.'

'I accept the challenge, Sir,' he'd replied. 'I shall ask for the captain's authorisation and I'll see for myself if it is really so terrible as you claim.'

The moment he was aboard I asked for the signal to steam out of the depot. We were well-stocked for the two days ahead, with tinned food, bread but especially water. Four or five litres of Algerian wine is fine for keeping up your spirits at a meal but we didn't touch a drop in the cab otherwise we wouldn't have got far!

To avoid dehydration we had three litres of water each, laced with coffee or a glass of arak.

I was concerned to see our lieutenant with his arms dangling by his side without any provisions whatsoever.

'I have brought nothing,' he said to me, 'since I have been informed that there is a buffet at Meidan. I return this evening as a passenger on the Turkish express.'

'Don't you worry,' I said. 'We've got six litres and there'll be enough for you.'

'I am like the camel, Sir,' he declared, standing erect. 'I drink but rarely.'

'Have it your own way, but you won't hold out. You'll end up having to drink.'

It was 35° in the shade when the express from Mosul pulled into the station. While the Turkish engine was being uncoupled I moved our engine to attach the restaurant car. I then coupled up the rest of the train and after checking the brakes I headed out for Mouslimiyé, our first stop on the road to Turkey. Like most engine crews me and my partner sucked either a small pebble or a cherry stone to keep our mouths moist.

Just after Mouslimiyé my partner had his first mouthful. I could stand it a bit longer since I wasn't stoking, but I soon grabbed the bottle and took my turn. When I offered it to the lieutenant, he refused, reminding me of his vow not to drink.

'Thank you Péroche, but I have already told you that I shall not drink.'

'We're not home yet lieutenant. You won't make it.'

We reached Ama station where two Syrians watered us and brought the coal forward. I took advantage of the halt to lubricate the bearings since the heat caused us to use a great deal of oil. Just before heading on I went to stick my head under the service water tap. My partner did the same. We opened the tap full and got a good dousing. We felt relatively fresh for the next half hour after this but then thirst set in again. Several times I proffered the bottle to the lieutenant but each time I was met with a refusal. All the same I felt that he was weakening. It was only his pride that stopped him telling us he was dying for a drink. After a while I decided to get angry.

'That's enough of this. You can't hold out. Drink!'

He looked at me, then sheepishly took the bottle. When he gave it back he was surprised to see that he had downed half a litre.

'And what about you?' he asked.

'Don't worry, there'll be enough.'

'It's terrible. I've never been so thirsty in my life,' he mumbled to himself.

We slogged up the steep gradients and I had to take the shovel to give my partner a breather. It was getting near midday, which brought with it the highest temperatures of the day. I sensed that the lieutenant was biting his tongue on seeing us cheerfully downing bottle after bottle.

'Have a drink mate,' I said. 'It's all right, we can stock up at Radjou.'

We pulled in with two minutes in hand and along with the three minutes stop we had a reasonable break. After filling the tender we managed to get three bottles of water. This would be enough to get us to Meida. At last we arrived at our destination and the engine was uncoupled and handed over to the depot watchman. Without even considering a wash we sped off for the buffet.

'Quick! To the boozer!'

And the lieutenant led the trio. On entering the buffet I gestured to the barman for a bottle of arak and several carafes of iced water.

'Is that for you?' exclaimed the lieutenant on seeing the bottle of arak.

I should add that he was a prime example of the extremely sober type.

'That's for us my young lieutenant. It won't do you any harm as long as you don't drink too much.' The lieutenant downed a good draught.

He didn't protest when I offered him another glass and he seemed to like it. It's true that his throat must have been parched. After we all washed up in the guard room he appeared to be more perky. His spirits were surely better than if he'd drunk mineral water.

We returned to the buffet where we enjoyed barbecued rabbit and potatoes. The lieutenant was hungry and I offered him a glass of Algerian wine to wash the rabbit down.

'I am afraid I am not accustomed to it, Sir and fear it may do me harm.'

'On the contrary! Wine like this makes your blood red.'

He seemed convinced.

After dinner we walked by the river to see the frontier and the chain of mountains silhouetted against the horizon. At the end of the day I went with the lieutenant to the station where he was to get the Orient Express back to Aleppo.

'I shall not forget this splendid journey with two black-faced fellows for the rest of my days,' he said, as he took his leave. 'I now have a better understanding of your task and the great spirit with which you accomplish it.' We shook hands as the train pulled out.

'Have a good trip lieutenant!'

After the war, I met this refined gentleman, with his high principles and warm heart, several times. He loved to recount the trip to the Turkish frontier and never tired of telling me his enjoyment of the experience.

The heat wasn't the only special thing about the country and French railwaymen were always coming across new surprises. One day in May, I was rostered, as usual, on my international express. I left Radjou station and accelerated up to 60 or 70 kilometres an hour. Suddenly, just coming off a bend I came face to face with an enormous flock of five or six hundred sheep. I slammed on the brakes but could do nothing to stop the train ploughing into the mass of livestock. The poor beasts rolled around the engine like balls of cotton wool. Most managed somehow to get off the track but on looking back I saw thirty or so littered around the rails.

The train went on at 20 kilometres an hour since the engine had not been damaged. As it was pointless to stop the train and lose thirty or forty minutes, I pushed her back up to the regular speed but with the smell of roast lamb wafting by. Once at Meidan I gave the engine a close inspection while she was taking on a full tank of water. Several grease pipes had been severed and others damaged but there was nothing serious. However, we had to give the front a hosing down with boiling water as it was spattered with sheep's blood. The incident was never mentioned by the train manager and that was the last we heard of the event.

Another surprising story took place at the Meidan depot at around seven in the morning. I was oiling the bearings while my crew mate cleaned the boiler. We were getting a move on since the sun rises at three and so was well up by seven. The water pump operator lived just facing the loco shed and as was usual in that country he fathered numerous children.

Two of his kids were sitting on a rug laid down in the

shade of the house with the younger one sucking on a baby's bottle. Suddenly we heard piercing shrieks. The operator's wife had spotted an enormous snake which was gliding straight at the children, probably drawn by the smell of milk.

The Syrian leapt up, grabbed a rifle and blasted at the animal which was only 15 metres from the kids. He hit the snake in the head and it jumped a metre high before dropping to the ground stone dead. It was as thick as my wrist and measured at least two metres. 'What a country!' I thought. 'This isn't the first time,' said the pump operator. 'The place is swarming with snakes.'

A few days later saw proof of his statement. The express used to arrive at one in the afternoon at Meidan and we'd usually take a stroll down by the river Karasu after our meal. That day the water seemed so tempting that I decided to take a dip along with a friend of mine from the Agen depot. I've got a lasting memory of a sort of long ribbon heading towards us when we were in mid river. It was a gigantic snake that was clearly not on a courtesy visit. I reckon that the fear it put into us made us get close to the world record for the 100 metres free style! When I got to the bank I swore I'd never splash about again in such hostile places.

I wouldn't want to give the impression that all the animals in the Karasu were man's enemies. At the end of May I was driving along the banks of the river with a head driver from Nimes that had joined us in the cab. On arrival, we noticed that something had made the Turkish border guards very excited. In fact, they had just caught an enormous carp, weighing at least thirty pounds, which gives you an idea of how old it was. The head driver loved fishing and the sight delighted him.

'If they're willing to sell it I'm more than willing to buy,' he said.

There was Syrian driver who used to work with us. He was close on sixty since retirement was a lot later there than in France. As he spoke Turkish very well he made his way towards the fishermen. They forded the river and came to parley over the carp. When they realised that the French soldiers wanted the fine fish they refused any notion of payment and were more than happy to offer it as a gift. Back at the buffet our *chef mécanicien* negotiated with the *chef de cuisine* to cook the carp for dinner. During the meal we toasted this friendly gesture of our Turkish friends, as was only right. I have to add that the centenary fish erased all my unpleasant memories of Syrian water snakes.

In late May some fairly dismal news came from France. The front had caved in and the Germans were marching on Paris. Weygrand had been called home and it was said he was doing his best to rectify the situation. The newsreels, highly optimistic as they were, talked only of French counter attacks, which were purely fictitious.

I learnt about the catastrophe in the early days of June. I was returning from the Turkish frontier with my express when a freight train passed on the up line at Ama station. The driver from the Niort depot shouted at me.

'The Germans have crossed the Loire and moving southeast.'

I didn't want to believe the news but it was confirmed when I pulled into Aleppo. An immense disappointment overcame us all.

Then it was the Armistice and General de Gaulle's appeal, which was broadcast several times on Radio Damascus and Radio Jerusalem. All these dramatic events provoked mayhem in the Middle East. Some career officers made their way to Palestine and used the English to try and get to London while others simply accepted defeat.

By the time Italy joined the war on the German side, 53 out of the 55 locos had arrived in Aleppo. The Italian railwaymen who were against the war had let the trains through and had treated our French comrades crewing them well. The railways form a family which takes no notice of frontiers as I would find out again later on several occasions. I took charge of my last train from Meidan to Aleppo at the end of June. On board this final Orient Express were the members of the Armistice Commission made up of Germans and Italians. At Aleppo station I saw 20 or 25 men, some in civilian dress, while others donned high military caps. These uniforms, unfortunately, would become familiar over the course of the following years. There were cars waiting to take them on to Damascus since it was not served by rail.

The war was well and truly over and there was nothing left for us to do in Syria. This said, we had to wait for three months before returning to France. There were tens of thousands of French soldiers stationed in the Middle East and we were all at a loose end, reduced to spending every evening at the cinema. Some picture houses showed only Arab films and we were not allowed in. Others were mixed but one side was for the military and the other for European civilians with the Arabs watching through the railings. These screened French, British and American films. Our favourite haunt was one run by the Catholic Circle, which had only high society clientele: officers, petty officers, company directors with their wives and children. Without being racist, in fact, it's very nice to find yourself among Frenchmen in a foreign country.

Nothing was more surprising than seeing the 8th Railway Brigade turning up to mass on a Sunday morning! The Catholic Circle was managed by a captain who had formerly been a priest in civvy street. He was a highly intelligent, generous man. Again and again he would say, 'The Circle is open to all, believers or not. You're all my flock as far as I'm concerned.'

I had friends who were communists and therefore anti-clerical but they were at home in the Circle and always pitched up first. We took advantage of the library, games and music, not to mention the bar where the drinks were very cheap. The captain had even planned a coach excursion to visit some holy shrines but the project came to nothing because of the Armistice.

Despite all this, time seemed to go by slowly with so little to do, and even more so since I was getting no letters from France. This silence worried me because a lot of my friends got mail regularly. I only discovered the explanation for this mystery when I returned to France. My wife had fallen for the rumours that some folk were spreading around: 'If you want your letters to get to Syria, they'll have to be posted in the Free Zone.'

As a result, she would give her envelopes regularly to the drivers running to Bordeaux so that they could pass them on to those entering the Free Zone. Funnily enough, these letters didn't get completely lost and some of them arrived on my doorstep several years after.

At the beginning of September, the Germans demanded that we should be repatriated urgently because of the shortage of railwaymen in France. But things weren't so simple. Ships were rare and the British were unchallenged masters of the Mediterranean. They checked methodically all vessels bound for France. As a consequence we considered crossing Europe on the Orient express, but the idea ran foul of the high command who didn't wish to be seen to show favour towards one category of servicemen over the others. To privilege railwaymen would have had a terrible effect on the troops' morale. And so we waited until the end of September to make the return voyage back to France.

The day we left was one of the luckiest spent in Syria. Many of us had been very sick in the previous months and the fever had even taken six or seven of our colleagues. In order to survive, the golden rule was to take quinine and those who didn't, did so at their own peril. I had never failed to take the precaution and probably this was why I hadn't been touched by the fever at all. But on the day prior to catching the train for the Lebanon I was shocked to find myself with a raging temperature and a terrible headache. I tried to hide my sickness and was careful not to cross the major for fear of being sent to hospital. If I were to miss this train my repatriation could well have been held up for a good while.

I downed some quinine, perhaps too much, and climbed aboard in the 40^0 heat. As I was barely conscious I thought that they would surely hospitalise me at Beirut. But a veritable miracle was in store. The fever went as fast as it had appeared. I got off the train as fresh as a daisy and tucked into a hearty breakfast, absolutely dumbfounded to be cured with such rapidity.

At Beirut we were driven back in trucks to the T2 barracks again. There, we had to wait another 10 days before boarding ship. At night on our straw mattresses we would listen to the howling jackals in the nearby mountain. In the daytime we frequented the restaurants, then we'd stroll around the town, calling in a bar sometimes. The railway company had awarded handsome premiums to train drivers and so we weren't short of money. I might even say that I was sitting on a small fortune since I had worked the most trains and, what's more, international expresses.

At last, one fine morning, we were told that the M.V. *Désirade* was weighing anchor the following day bound for France. Our joy was indescribable at the news. We already smelt home in the air. Everyone was on board on schedule but the departure was postponed on account of the British. In fact the ship was mixed. Not only was it carrying soldiers and those being repatriated from Syria but also goods which the Germans could profit from in France. The British message was that if the vessel left with any supplies such as horses and grain it would be torpedoed.

The French authorities bent to these demands and finally the *Désirade* steamed out of Beirut harbour at around six in the evening. Night had fallen as we moved away slowly, as if regretfully, from the Lebanese capital, illuminated by thousands of flickering specks of light.

Although we had crossed the Mediterranean at top speed on the voyage out, the return journey was very different. Before the Armistice the French navy used good quality coal, usually from Britain, but now it had to make do with coal dust from the Massif Central. It formed clinker and slag and it was necessary to clean out the fire every seven or eight hours.

It was also a danger of a different sort on the return voyage. Going out we had to steam with all lights out to elude the Germans. Going back all the decks were bathed in light for fear of the British. All night, powerful spotlights were beamed on a large banner strung between the funnels on which was written the word 'FRANCE'.

The day after we set sail, in mid-afternoon, we were admiring the deep blue of the Mediterranean and lolling on the ship rails when a British aircraft homed in on us and emitted flashes. We knew at once that it was morse. It flashed three times and my friend next to me deciphered it as, 'Stop and await further orders.'

The *Désirade* stopped engines at once. Before the arrival of the search party, bags of mail (no doubt compromising) were burnt in the boiler room. The passengers, however, had to wait until evening before they saw the superstructure and funnels of a British cruiser. An hour later the vessel drew up alongside and several British officers climbed up the embarkation ladder. They went through the ship from stem to stern and left after about an hour without giving any further instructions. We were drifting with the current since the anchor was useless in such deep waters. Suddenly the plane reappeared and signalled in Morse, 'Continue on your course.' The engines turned over again and the *Désirade* headed west.

Just as on the outward voyage, the commissioned and warrant officers dined together, but this time I couldn't sneak in my friend from Saint-Mariens. Luckily the food for the servicemen was far better than that on the *Patria*. Restrictions there were, but the meals were copious and the food excellent. If the coal was second grade then we could still count on our sweet bread rolls, croissants, chocolate and delicious drinks.

The ship plodded on slowly at 7 or 8 knots as far as Crete. There, instead of heading north and crossing the Ionian Sea, the ship held south and ended up just off the port of Bizerte, five days after leaving Beirut. No one knew why we were there and when we would leave even less. It was the deepest of mysteries. To pass the days we swam in the turquoise sea and strolled through the Tunisian town.

At last, after a weeks' wait, we received the order to weigh anchor at midnight. No sooner had the captain heard this than he took on fine quality coal and stores for his passengers – fruit, meat, fish and wine. A pilot took us down the channel and without even stopping our ship he jumped across into his pilot boat and waved us farewell. To the surprise of all, the *Désirade* turned westwards instead of heading north.

The ship moored off the port of Bône, in the Constantine district, so as to join a convoy leaving Algeria the following morning. The coal we had taken on at Bizerte meant we could steam at a fair clip and thanks to the stores taken on at the same time we were sure not to die of hunger.

On the other hand, we brushed with death for the rest of the voyage. The captain had been told to follow the Italian coast and keep a check on his position by signals with the land since some waters had been mined. In the middle of the night one of our convoy, which was transporting North African troops back to France, struck a mine. There were several casualties, while some were drowned or reported missing.

The survivors were picked up and we continued warily, hugging the Italian coastline. Instead of passing through the straits of Bonifacio, a route which would have shortened our journey considerably, we sailed through the Gulf of Genoa so as to keep to the French coast. The *Désirade* passed Toulon harbour and soon steamed into the Port of Marseilles. We were now in early October and the Syrian climate was a long way behind us. It was cool and there were thick mists. After eight months we stepped onto the soil of our blood-stained, defeated homeland.

The railwaymen of the southwest stayed only a couple of days in the Saint-Marthe camp. They left for Nimes and from there headed for Millau to be de-mobbed. I handed in my military gear and received the khaki civilian outfit, which had been specially produced for those being repatriated. It was called 'The Pétain suit.' The day after we arrived in Millau I was taking an early walk in the countryside along with some friends, when a group of peasants, who were already at work, invited us to help them harvesting grapes. We accepted gladly, and received two good meals in return. Eating in the company of these generous Midi folk, strangely we felt neither gloom nor sadness.

Four days later the Germans authorised a convoy to Bordeaux. A special train was arranged made up of sixteen large metal-sided coaches. The compartment walls had been removed thus allowing 2,000 repatriated soldiers to be carried. As a sergeant I was in charge of a coachload of men. After messing on tins of sardines, bully beef and pâté the men sat down in the coach. We had nothing to drink but fortunately we spent only one night in these conditions. The men in my coach were virtually all survivors of the ship that had been mined off Italy and had saved nothing apart from their lives.

We pulled into Langon, the demarcation line, around midday. Four very serious-faced Prussians checked our coach. They hastened to look over the papers of all the passengers. However, when they learnt that it was a train of railwaymen they skipped all the formalities. At half past ten we were in good old Bordeaux.

As we had two hours to spare before our train to Nantes we decided to have a look around the town. We very quickly discovered that restrictions were the order of the day. There was beer, soft drinks and mineral water but, alas, not a drop of wine. At the baker's we were asked for ration coupons and we had to explain where we had come from before we were allowed to buy bread. We quickly became acquainted with the occupation. Luckily we still had some tins of army rations that we ate in the guard room of Saint Jean station.

It was there that I came across the guard with whom I had passed the grim Christmas night of 1938 in Lormont tunnel. He came from Saintes and knew my family well. He told me that my brother, also an engine driver but in Aceres, had been taken prisoner. My parents, on the other hand, were well. Just after I met the guard of the Saint Mariens train who gave me news of my wife and daughter After five months of silence and worry I was relieved at last.

I took the 12.30 express and arrived at Saint Mariens three quarters of an hour later. Our feet had barely touched the platform when all our old railway friends and those working in the station buffet fell upon us.

'We didn't think you'd ever come. You cut a fine figure Péroche in your Pétain gear!'

The train pulled out while all this was going on but my friends left aboard recognised my wife in the garden as the train went by. By gesticulating from the window they signalled to her that I was home. She understood immediately and ran down to the station to see me.

'I never thought I'd see you again,' she said breathlessly. It was an unforgettable moment that I feel is impossible to put into words.

'Come and see Madeleine,' she went on.

I accompanied her to our home. Antoinette woke up the sleeping child. I found her very much changed. She was a little over two and her hair had grown. She looked at me but failed to recognise who I was.

'It's your papa,' explained Antoinette.

'Papa!' she repeated, holding out her tiny arms.

Chapter 6
The Fusible Plugs

THE GERMAN occupation totally upset the running of the Saint Mariens depot. Some regular services to Coutras, Libourne, Chateauneuf, Saintes and Bordeaux continued, but the German trains took priority over everything. The traffic from Blaye, for instance, was dense because of the need to transport petrol; similarly, there were a good many munitions trains from Bedenec and Jonzac.

The German railwaymen managed all the stations and took over the running of trains and allocation of locomotives. In fact, we preferred to work with them rather than with the military who were simply blind brutes, drunk with success. For sure, our colleagues from across the Rhine were in France as occupants, but they were always reasonable and understanding with their French counterparts.

During the first days of the occupation I was relieved of duty by the regional office to rest up. For me, this was a joke since I had just spent four months doing almost nothing. Still, I jumped at the chance to see my parents at Saintes and meet up with my friends again. The depot was very busy and after this break I felt fit as ever and threw myself back into my work

My return to duty was highlighted by a frightful story full of twists and turns. I'll give the facts as objectively as I can before recounting all the ramifications of the affair.

It was the end of October 1940 and I was heading a works train which left Saint Mariens around six in the morning and came back from Bordeaux at seven in the evening. On the day concerned, my fireman was an apprentice driver, so he knew the job. The previous day the *chef de réserve* had asked me to do him a favour.

'Look, since you'll be in Bordeaux all day, can you pick up a suit for me? It's at the tailor's on rue Sainte Catherine.'

'Of course I can if that helps you out.'

'Thanks a lot. I'll see you at the station.'

The run to Bordeaux went without a hitch. We'd just reached Roche sur Yon and the engine was running fairly well. All the same, you could feel that she wasn't in top condition, mainly because maintenance wasn't carried out scrupulously in those days. I went to pick up the *chef's* suit in the afternoon and stowed it in the chest at the rear of the tender.

We steamed out of Bordeaux on time and arrived at Saint André de Cubzac with the water gauge on three quarters and steam enough to spare. We could take on the 12% gradient without a worry.

All of a sudden, half way up the grade, my partner sensed something was wrong as he was stoking the fire.

'I can hear a leak in the firebox,' he said worriedly. I leaned forward and took a look.

'I can't see anything, but you're right. I can certainly hear a leak. Still, it's probably just coming from a smoke tubes. We'll try to make it to Saint Mariens all the same.'

With a new charge of coal in the firebox the noise got much louder and much more worrying. At Aubie Saint Antoine station I had to brake sharply since we were still doing 80 kilometres an hour. I opened the firebox door and saw right away that the leak wasn't coming from a smoke tube at all, but from the crown plate. That could only mean that it was one of the fusible plugs.

'It can't have melted for lack of water', I said. 'The injector's feeding the boiler on maximum.'

'That's right Marcel. And even if there is a leak, the glass is on half.'

Usually when the fusible plugs melt, they go so fast that it's like a gun going off. The steam comes out of two holes each two centimetres wide at 15 kilos a square centimetre.

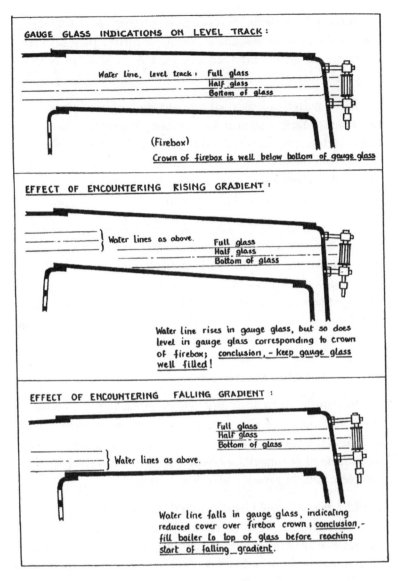

GAUGE GLASS INDICATIONS ON LEVEL TRACK:

Water line, level track: Full glass
Half glass
Bottom of glass

(Firebox)
Crown of firebox is well below bottom of gauge glass

EFFECT OF ENCOUNTERING RISING GRADIENT:

Water lines as above. Full glass
Half glass
Bottom of glass

Water line rises in gauge glass, but so does
level in gauge glass corresponding to crown
of firebox; conclusion, - keep gauge glass
well filled!

EFFECT OF ENCOUNTERING FALLING GRADIENT:

Full glass
Half glass
Bottom of glass

Water lines as above.

Water line falls in gauge glass, indicating
reduced cover over firebox crown; conclusion,-
fill boiler to top of glass before reaching
start of falling gradient.

Diagram of
water level
(Courtesy P.
Semmens
*How Steam
Locomotives
Really Work*)

What's more, the plugs blow when the engine's on an incline
or on the level yet we had noticed it going downhill. [1]

(1) 'Being at one end of the boiler, the indication can alter
considerably with the changing gradient. For instance, the
glass on one of Gresley's A4 Pacifics is 165 mm high. On level
track, with water at the bottom of the glass, there is a
covering of 121 mm. over the back of the inner firebox, which
corresponds to only 57 mm over the fusible plug at the front.
However, on a rising gradient of 1 in 57, with the water level
at the same point in the glass, the cover at the front of the
firebox decreases to zero.' Semmens & Goldfinch p. 70.

Although we dropped the fire on stopping, it was too late. The water was now streaming out of the melted plug hole and the water gauge had slumped to zero. This caused the second plug to blow.

Faced with this I signaled for help from up the line – that is from Saint Mariens station. Our passengers got out and gazed at the lifeless, pressure-less and fire-less engine. Some of them grumbled a bit since they'd be an hour late for dinner. But as for me, I was stupefied – even more so as I simply couldn't understand what lay behind the affair.

The rescue loco steamed in and hauled our engine and the coaches to Saint Mariens. I've no need to describe the reception we got there from the *chef de réserve* and the *chef mécanicien*. The former took his new suit before listening to our explanation. Nevertheless, they were both my friends; in fact, I'd even worked alongside the *chef mécanicien*. They listened to my story without interrupting. However, I felt, deep down they were still skeptical. How could a fusible plug possibly melt when the crown plate was covered with water?

To claim such an absurdity flew in the face of every basic safety mechanism of a steam engine. No one wanted to believe or defend me and it was clear that I'd have to bear the consequences of this major offence. At the same time I had complete faith in myself and a clear conscience.

Back home I could hardly eat a thing and didn't sleep a wink all night. In '36 when Henri IV and I were on the famous Royan-Paris express we could have blown the damned plugs a hundred times. In those days we were, brass-necked daredevils but Lady Luck had always been there to save us from catastrophe. On this occasion she'd cruelly let us down.

The blow was particularly bad for my partner, the apprentice driver, whose career was now unfairly in the balance. Still, I said to myself in the darkness, that's life.

The next day the boss gave me a full accident report form to fill in – the sinister Form 53. I wrote exactly what had happened without leaning on excuses. Since the 53 form had been introduced drivers and firemen alike had always searched for 'extenuating circumstances'.

The verdict came the same morning in the form of a telephone call from the regional office. The two guilty parties were to be stood down from driving duty for three months. That was the standard regulatory outcome. The administrative punishment had to be discussed and would come later. The engine was parked off limits and the shed door locked and sealed.

We should have been posted in the engine repair shops but the severe shortage of engine crews spared us this and we were put on engine preparation duty and engine crew replacement working from four in the afternoon to midnight.

The inquiry should have taken place with the regional repair inspector, the *chef de réparations* at Saint Mariens, the *chef de réserve* and of course the engine driver concerned. When the regional inspector arrived by express from Saintes I was busy greasing a locomotive. He had only recently been posted to the region and, I guessed, was between 35 and 40.

He was wearing a well cut suit and walked smartly over to the *chef de réserve*'s office. Half an hour later he appeared alongside the *chef de réserve* but wearing blue overalls. They made their way over to the engine where the *chef de réparations* was waiting. The two experts looked inside the boiler while the *chef de réserve* stayed on the footplate. The minutes ticked by and still they didn't send for me. I began to be a little mystified. At last the two emerged from the boiler, picked up their colleague waiting on the footplate and headed back to the office in heated discussion. It was impossible that the inspection had finished. The main party, that means us, the accused, hadn't even been with them. Just before midday the inspector was back in his suit. He had lunch in the buffet and left for Saintes on the three o' clock train.

I decided to make my astonishment known to my boss.

'So why was I left out of the inquiry then? What about the rules? The driver and the fireman are supposed to be there at the inspection.'

'The inspector thought it best not to send for you. Don't worry the boiler's not damaged. The plugs will be replaced this afternoon and the engine can be fired up tomorrow.'

And that's exactly what happened. The engine was put back in service with new plugs. When the injectors were tested before our eyes they worked perfectly. The mystery thickened and as we were to discover later, there were more surprises to come.

The sanction came a few days later. Apart from three months standing down, the standard censure involved a reprimand from the Paris chief and retention of several months bonus. However, all we received was a reprimand from the *chef d'arrondissement*, which was far less serious, and the symbolic retention of one months bonus. For sure, it was a pleasant surprise, but there was a question that wouldn't go away. Why didn't we get the statutory sanction?

We would have to wait a fair while before that question was answered.

We continued to clock in at four in the morning to prepare the locomotives or to drive the replacement engines. We felt very awkward when our friends asked us about the accident and made do with a shrug of the shoulders.

'Three months won't be long,' they'd say.

One November morning, just after the service mail had arrived the *chef de réserve* rushed out of his office with his black coat flying in the autumn wind.

'Péroche, come to my office. I've had a message about you.'

'What is it now?' I groaned. 'Nothing good, that's for sure.'

He held out a note which read as follows: The regional office hereby requests that Driver Péroche and passed fireman X shall be returned to duties. They shall be allocated a dedicated locomotive and they are to be integrated in the regular A service.

I was flabbergasted. I stared at my boss.

'I don't understand anything any more. We've been stood down for twenty days instead of three months. Why?'

'Let's say I'm just pleased for you Péroche. Take the 4-6-0.'

The whole depot was amazed at the decision. Such a thing had never been seen before.

Some days later the *chef de traction* came to give a presentation and my boss told me that I was to attend. I knew the speaker well since he'd been my *chef mécanicien* at Thouars. At the end of his presentation he gestured for me to join him.

'What happened was just unbelievably bad luck,' he said. 'I can't tell you the extenuating circumstances regarding the meltdown of the plugs, as you can imagine. But you still have our trust as well as that of the *chef d'arrondissement*. The proof is that you're back in the cab well before the three months are up.'

'That's all very well. But can't you give me some details? Up until now I've been left in the dark.'

'No questions. Your bosses think it best you're reinstated for service, full stop. That's it. Don't even try to understand. Do your job conscientiously, as you've always done, and soon this affair will be just a bad memory. I promise you that it won't be on your record.'

He'd shed a glimmer of light on this mystery, but I was still very confused all the same. All my bosses were unusually kind to me and spoke to me in a way they'd never done before. Well, let things alone I said to myself and we'll see what happens.

Life retuned to normal and the memory of the affair faded. Then, in February 1941 my boss sent for me.

'Péroche,' he said, 'you've been selected by the district to take the advanced training course at Le Mans for fast trains and expresses. You're to attend the next session starting March 1st for a month.'

'You're joking!'

'Not at all.'

'But to do the course you can't have a serious reprimand on your record. Which is not my case.'

'Oh come on Péroche! I've explained all that.'

'I'm not going to Le Mans. Just leave me alone.'

'Come come now! Don't refuse this whatever you do. It's your future you're playing with. Be reasonable man!'

'There's nothing you can do. I'm not going and that's it.'

'Very well. Put your refusal in writing and give your reasons.'

It was a poisoned chalice they were offering. I had a lot to lose and not much to gain. The course was very hard and in the end they only let ten through out of a good thirty candidates. I was at a disadvantage compared to those drivers who came from the professional college at Nantes or the SNCF's second degree school of apprentices.

My chances to get up with the first ten were slim and I'd no wish to be shown up as a dunce. However, what my bosses said was true. Even if I didn't pass, I'd learn something new. What's more the SNCF paid a lot for these courses. You were on full wages and expenses without actually producing anything for a month.

When my friends heard about my decision they all tried to make me change my mind.

'Take it Marcel! You won't get another chance. It's not often they choose passed drivers to go on the course. Usually it's apprentice drivers they choose to guarantee them express drivers for a longer period. If you refuse, it'll go down on your record. Come on Péroche don't let this chance slip by.'

I accepted at the last minute. At worst, as I said, I'd learn something. The love of the job got the better of my pride.

So on 1st March, I enrolled at this famous college at Le Mans that we'd heard so much about, along with a colleague from Saint Mariens. The courses were given by a highly eminent divisional inspector. However, it appeared that he wasn't beyond criticism. First, he often used technical terms that were beyond the reach of his classes, which weren't made up of polytechnicians and second, he was extremely sardonic. When one of the class got lost because he hadn't understood,

The roundhouse at Le Mans just before World War II. The photo gives an idea of the size of the depot (La Vie du Rail)

he'd mock him and then ignore him completely. This man, with such a great mind appeared to delight in the mistakes of others and he'd never think to help them. What's more he was a football fanatic. We all had to play football with him during the breaks. I was bored by this since I was no good at it. Consequently he assigned me to goalkeeper where I didn't do too badly in fact.

The part of the course relating to the engines, braking systems and test trains was given by a traction inspector, who was a completely different kettle of fish. He was a serious man, very distant, less intellectual but more on our level. He was highly demanding and a miser with his marks. He would hear nothing of sports. For him only the railways counted. He'd even make us attend in the evening after the canteen to go over the course. Sometime this could last until 11 at night. He was forever saying, 'The SNCF has done a lot for you, so take advantage of this course and work hard while you have the chance.'

After a week of listening to regulations and loco mechanics I thought I was going crazy. Some relaxation was called for. Consequently a friend and myself decided to go to the pictures after dinner one evening. On coming out of the cinema we took the train at Le Mans station to return to our lodgings at the depot guard room. But fate was against us. The first face we saw in our coach was that of the work-fanatic inspector.

'Well, well! Where have you two sprung from?'

'From the cinema Sir,' we answered in all honesty.

'And what about your course work?'

'In fact we couldn't take any more and decided to have a change for the evening.'

He understood how we felt and relaxed. He told us that the SNCF had assigned him as advisor for the production of the film *La Bête Humaine*. [2]

'You know,' he said, 'Jean Gabin has only done one or two scenes on real trains. It's one of your men who's the driver for most of the time. My job is to to check and coordinate what he does with Gabin's movements so that the whole thing looks believable.'

So our little escapade ended up with a lively discussion and the inspector turned out to be a real talker.

But we weren't at Le Mans to chat about films. The four weeks were devoted to regulations, signalling, locomotives and braking systems. Then there were the exams which enabled them to give you a mark. What we already knew was expanded on and we learnt new ideas with the help of diagrams representing all the various types of engines and there were also training films.

Right from the first week the traction inspector took us out on the training engines to see what we knew about being a fireman and driver. The day before we took an engine out we'd be told the number of our Pacific and we had to give it an inspection. It was parked over an inspection pit and the whole point of the exercise was to spot the anomalies that had been set up.

On the following day the lord high traction inspector

---

(2) Jean Renoir's classic film about engine driver Jacques Lantier (played by Jean Gabin). *La Bête Humaine* has footage from the cab of Lantier's Pacific. It also gives a good idea of the daily routine of an engine driver in the 1930s.

arrived with his chamois leather gloves. We'd made sure to give the cab a good clean and polish the windows.

He shook hands and asked: 'Everything in order? Have you been round the engine?'

'Yes Sir.'

'Well Péroche what did you find?'

'A good few things. Missing pieces, split pins that had dropped out, loose bearings and connecting rods and wedges from the wheel boxes resting on the springs.'

'And what have you done about them?'

'I noted the needed repairs in the maintenance log and they were carried out immediately.'

'Very good. Now, let's get on the road.'

The dedicated driver requested the signal to leave the depot then proceeded to couple up the Paris-Nantes-Quimper express, which consisted of 14 coaches or a load of 812 tonnes. The load may seem enormous for a Pacific but the line wasn't demanding and under the occupation the trains didn't travel very fast. When we were due to leave the driver and fireman went back and got aboard the guard's van. The inspector then called out the first two trainees.

'You are to take the train to the Anger halt. Of course I'll give you all you need to know about the line because you're not familiar with it.'

Despite a fairly easy track, things didn't go too well for the first two colleagues. The engine steamed well but the water feed was poor and there was something wrong with the pump so they had to keep using the injector. [3] On arrival at Anger there were only 3 centimetres of water in the tube. The inspector gave a moan.

While the water was being taken on I got hold of a spanner and climbed down. I unscrewed the filter cap of the water

---

(3) Initially, water was supplied to the boiler through a mechanical water-feed pump which kept the level up automatically. Injectors were brought in to supply water when the engine was stationary and the feed mechanism obviously stopped.

pump and found it was blocked with strands of hemp from the end of the water tower hose and bits of coal. After giving it a good clean, I replaced the filter and screwed back the cap.

When the train pulled out the inspector could see that the pump was working better and that the feed was back to normal. With a smile on his face he tapped my shoulder.

'I'll remember your intervention at Anger Péroche. A good move to clean the filter.'

I made a mental note of it.

'And now' he said, 'take the regulator.'

I obeyed and took charge until Nantes without any problems. The dedicated team took back their engine to steam into the depot and afterwards we headed for the canteen.

On the return run the inspector took the train out and asked two new trainees to look after the regulator and the fire. Unfortunately the fireman trainee was based in a small depot and had never had the opportunity to drive a Pacific. Things went from bad to worse since we had already lost a few minutes on the trip to Angers.

'Grab a shovel Péroche!' the inspector snapped as he took over the regulator. 'Let's see if we can get out of this.'

While we were taking on water at Angers we brought thirty or so bricks forward and broke them in order to build up the fire. Although the glass was only half full, the last leg of the journey went smoothly and we pulled up in Le Mans on time. While I was washing down I thought about the day and decided that it had not been time wasted.

However I may have celebrated my victory prematurely. In the third week of the course I twisted my ankle at football. It swelled terribly but I could continue attending the classes. During ther breaks I swopped the round ball for books and revised rules and regulations conscientously.

At last it was the final week and the exams. On Monday at nine the divisional inspector led us into the examination hall and announced with his habitual ironic humour.

'With whom shall we commence? Ah! Why not Péroche! You haven't been distracted by football for a while, you can go first.'

The least you can say is that I didn't feel like a spoilt child. It would have been far better to be tested on Friday after improving your answers from all the others. Still, I suppose someone's got to be first.

I stood up and joined the inspector in front of the blackboard. The decor was complimented by drawings and diagrams of machines and brake mechanisms. Despite all my fears it must have been my lucky day since I knew the answer to every question that was asked. I should add that the divisional inspector behaved reasonably for once. He kept his derision to himself and didn't tempt me into making errors. At half past ten the other inspector took me onto a Pacific and asked me to get her underway, an exercise similar to that I had on the test train. He ordered me to halt the distribution on one side then isolate the engine from the tender. He tested me on the triple valves, the auxiliary reservoirs and the braking cylinders. In short, he kept me busy.

By twelve o' clock it was all over. What a relief! With a free spirit I could now watch the others for the rest of the week. It would have been better to have answered the questions alone with the inspector because sometimes being in front of the class sapped your confidence. The inspector couldn't stop himself sometimes making comments that had the rest of the class in stitches. I later found out that these jokes, however, were not random. In fact, we were marked on our reaction to a colleague in trouble and other situations that were engineered during the exams.

The two inspectors and the whole class finished the month-long course with a communal dinner in the SNCF canteen. And then it was farewell. I took the train with my friend from Saint Mariens, who had also done satisfactorily over the month.

'My mind's easy,' he said.

'Yes,' I added, 'I'm fairly pleased that we came through the course. I don't reckon I'll be in the first ten, but I won't be too far below. The main thing is that we didn't make a fool of ourselves.'

It was mid April. I'd just clocked at the depot to go to Blaye when my boss gave me a shout.

'Péroche! Congratulations!'

'What?'

'I've just got your marks from Le Mans. They're excellent. You came sixth out of thrity four.'

'I looked at him speechless and stupefied. I could hardly believe it. '

'Read it,' he said.

There it was in black and white. I had come sixth with 17 out of 20. The citation finished with the following phrase: Péroche, Marcel is hereby authorised to drive fast and express trains and, after a induction course, to join the Pacific service.

'Well then *chef*. I think we'd better drink to that eh!'

I was called a few days later to attend a course at Rochelle. The moment I arrived I was booked into the regular service with a driver-instructor and his dedicated engine – a Pacific in excellent condition. My instructor was a fine driver who later became a close friend. He gave me no end of good advice as we ran links to Poitiers, Nantes and Bordeaux.

The only black spot during this period concerned food. The Rochelle depot didn't have a canteen and my hours were so tight that I didn't have time to do any shopping. To make things worse I only got back to Saint Mariens on a Sunday. I've never eaten so many sardines in my life!

Luckily my mother was on good terms with a grocer in Saint-Eutrope street and managed to help me out with some tinned food. At Rochelle a cousin on my wife's side also gave me something. She queued up for me to get some black pudding or some meat at a butcher's she knew. Lastly, like all folk from Rochelle, my friends had as much fish as they could eat. I felt a bit awkward being on the receiving end of such generosity but work and family ties get closer during a war or food shortage. What's more, the moment I climbed into the cab of my Pacific to reach for the regulator, food and other problems faded away. I was as black as a jackdaw and dog tired after long hours – but always ready for another 100 kilometres, with my head stuck out of the cab window and the wind in my face.

Before the end of the course I had to drive two more test trains to become one of the *élite*. There were two examiners. The first was a real smart character, 'hail friend well met' type and all of us assumed he was on our side. The second was strict, remote and friendless. He wasn't the type to do any of us an injustice but he'd do nothing to help you either. I obviously got the second.

However, although he was very cold and said little I have no criticisms. I headed a Rochelle-Poitiers up train during the day and the down at night in perfect conditions. Then he made me carry out a close inspection of the engine. Without a word between us we each drew up an inventory of repairs needed. Then we compared our lists.

'That's very good,' he said. 'Your test trains were fine. I'll recommend a pass to the district office.'

He kept to his word. Ten days later I got the official certificate from Paris. What a story! Six months before I was put at the bottom of the class: the blot on my copy book was the most serious transgression that a railway driver could commit. Then by May 1941 I was suddenly out of the doldrums and at the summit of the profession. From that day on I was considered as a top-class driver, a record white as the driven snow. I had become a Pacific senator.

Today, the war's now a long way off and there are no steam engines working in France. Consequently I can unlock the mystery of the famous fusible plugs as it was told to me some years after by one of the railway inspectors who had taken part in the inquiry.

It has to be said, first of all, that where steam engines are concerned, be they railway or marine, the biggest drawback is the scale that builds up in the boiler. This varies according to how hard the water supply is. Before Armand's invention for descaling, all the boilers had to cleaned every eight days or so with high pressure boiling water. The fusible plugs were cleaned, removed, checked and replaced with new ones if there was the slightest anomaly. Moreover, it was essential to put acid in the water tender. This helped to minimise the scaling on the inner surface of the boiler in general and the crown plate in particular. Depending on which region you were working you used the chemical in solid or liquid form. Usually it was the fireman who actually added the chemical to the water but always on the orders of the driver.

Nevertheless it has to be remembered that we were at war. The 4-6-2 engine 040 was originally from La Roche-sur-Yonne and so would have been under the Nantes office. Before coming to Saint Mariens, however, she had taken part in the exodus of the French from Brittany. In short, during this painful period of our history many railwaymen were mobilised and others simply disappeared to avoid the call up. It was chaos. The engines were poorly maintained and when the boilers were washed the plugs were sometimes missed and sometimes not checked. When the loco arrived at Saint Mariens, the Germans were demanding trains every day to move their fuel and munitions. Consequently, she was put straight into service without a maintenance check.

At the inquiry one of the men working in the yard overheard an inspector say, 'The bastards! Damned bastards.

To whom was he referring? The fireman? The driver? No. In fact he has referring to those who had failed to maintain the engine because of the war. They had found the boiler completely covered in scale with a thick layer on the crown plate. The fusible plugs were almost totally encrusted in scale.

On the fateful day in October 1940 I had added two two blocks of descalant on the up run and two more on the return journey from Bordeaux. This double dose had loosened the scale on the crown plate. Since it was a suburban train the engine was continually stopping and starting. The scaling around the fusible plugs therefore, had been three quarters eaten away and had given in to the pressurised boiling water. That was why the plugs started to leak on an incline. The second plug, which had stayed intact, gave way once all the water had escaped through the first plug hole even though we had dropped the fire.

We had been the victims of an incredible string of circumstances but we had risked a hell of a lot more than a three month stand down. During the 1914-18 war a similar accident occurred at Rochelle on an American TP. Fresh water was rare at that time and the loco was using sea water. The boiler wasn't scaled with calcium but salt, which was far more dangerous. One day the salt, which had formed a crust on the crown plate cracked. The water then leaked through the fissures. The water in the boiler was suddenly exposed to the full heat of the crown plate and became superheated. The safety valves simply could not cope with the extra pressure and the boiler exploded. The driver and fireman were blown to smithereens. To obtain an idea of the blast the pieces of the locomotive were scattered as far as one kilometre away. Such a fate may well have awaited our 4-6-0.

Once the inspector realised what had happened he decided not to allow me into the inquiry, otherwise things would have turned out differently. It was my right to insist on being present at the inquiry and the inspection but something inside me told me it was better to do nothing. Since I had committed no fault I had a clear conscience. With the benefit of hindsight I thank Providence that I acted as I did. If I had pressed my case then the depots at La Roche sur Yonne and Saint Mariens would have been dragged into the affair, not to mention the two district offices at Nantes and Saintes. Far easier for my bosses to find two scapegoats. In the end such a flagrant injustice worked in my favour as my superiors were silently grateful and never forgot how my silence made their lives a lot easier. After the war my 12th month bonus was restored and the affair was erased from my file. In short, I was held in greater esteem by them after this frightful event.

Bomb damage at Cherbourg
(La Vie du Rail)

Chapter 7
Under the German Yoke

T HE WAR widened and 1941 saw the invasion of Russia by Hitler's troops and the entry of the US against Japan and Germany. The conflict looked set to be a long one, and we would not be free from the German yoke for a while yet. The Germans now planned to fortify the west of France by constructing the famous Atlantic Wall. [1] To complete this mammoth task they understood that the key would be transport. The staff of the Western Region were clearly insufficient and so a call was put out for drivers and firemen from the southwest, meaning Thouars, Bressuire, Niort, Rochelle, Saintes and Saint-Mariens.

It may appear idiotic to reduce staff at the Saint-Mariens depot when staffing was already tight, but in times of war, economic considerations take second place. Moreover, for the sake of fairness, the district order was for all depots to supply men. In those areas classed as 'danger' or 'red' zones locomotives were frequently strafed or bombed. What's more, resistance sabotage sometimes led to derailments. As a consequence it was only fair that the risks should be shared out evenly and in fact, nobody spoke out against the policy.

At the end of 1941 it was my turn. I was to leave with a fine friend who was a fireman I'd trained up years ago. We arrived at Auray depot on the Bordeaux-Quimper train and were set to work immediately. We were to drive the sand trains in the Quiberon peninsula where the famous wall was being raised.

---

(1) The Atlantic Wall was not a continuous structure but intermittent strategic defences. Nevertheless it took 11m tonnes of concrete, 1m tonnes of steel and 450,000 impressed workers.

The most vivid memory of my first stay in Brittany was an incredibly violent night when the disasters of war were compounded by a horrific railway accident. My partner and I had finished work and were parked on a sideline near Carnac station, waiting for our relief crew due on the passenger train from Auray. At around 8 at night we heard a horrendous crash coming from the station. A signaling error had allowed a locomotive, steamed up and ready to head a train to Auray to be rammed by a workers' train. In the coaches damaged by the impact we pulled out the dead and wounded. By sheer luck, the two traction men coming to relieve us had been spared the tragedy since they were traveling at the rear of the train and were only dazed.

Before we could leave for Auray, a 50-ton crane had to be sent for to shift the engines and the derailed rolling stock from the track. All four of us were huddled in the cab waiting, with the fire door open to keep us warm. We were nodding off when suddenly we were woken up by the drone of incoming British aircraft and for the first time I witnessed a heavy air raid. The planes dropped their bombs on Lorient in successive waves and the sky was lit up by the tracers of the German antiaircraft fire. After this outburst of flashes and explosions the aircraft made off and silence returned. However, the night sky was lit up by the incendiaries raging in the martyred city.

When my time in the red zone was over I returned to Saint-Mariens, but it was merely a respite and I was back there again in May 1942.

This second posting started under the worst auspices. The crew we were to replace and who were to meet us to give us details of the road we were to work, didn't show up at Saint-Mariens at the given time. We had no news of our two comrades and their families began to get worried. Then we heard the reason for the delay. They were in the hands of the Gestapo.

In Audierne bay, with its famous Ekhmul lighthouse, the Germans had decided to take the sand from the huge beach, stock it and then transport it by 800 ton double-headed trains. To do this, they had built 25 kilometres of track between Treguennec and Pont l'Abbé. On the day they were due to come home, our two relief crew had climbed aboard their engine, which had been steamed and was ready to leave for Pont l'Abbé. From there, they were due to travel back to Saint-Mariens. A few minutes after they had started off, the Breton resistance blew up a bridge. The Gestapo were furious and arrested all the railwaymen in the area. Our two comrades were among them.

The SNCF representatives did everything they could to obtain their release from prison, but they came up against total refusal.

'They'll be tried along with the rest . . .' was the only answer they obtained.

Fortunately the German rail authorities stepped in. They had a large say in what went on, even with the army, since the military clearly recognised that transport was one of the main arteries of the war.

'Go on! Lock up all the French railwaymen,' the German railway bosses used to say, 'especially the drivers, and you can take their places!'

The Nazi police saw reason, but before releasing them, forced them to sign a document stating that they would be arrested should they be involved in sabotage a second time. It was the sword of Damocles hanging over them for the entire war and for this reason the conflict must have seemed that much longer for them.

So our two friends turned up three days late. I must admit my partner and I weren't exactly over the moon to replace them. We saw ourselves already in prison since the Bretons were giving stiff resistance to the occupation. Our only hope of escaping the Pont l'Abbé duty was the Quimper *chef de feuille*, who was an old friend. I remembered well when this young engineer from *Arts et Metiers* had been doing his fireman's apprenticeship and had been assigned to me.

'Don't you worry,' I said to my partner. 'I'll ask him to keep us based on the Quimper depot. We'll work the trains for Quimperlé or Chateaulin rather than working for the German's in that God-forsaken Audierne Bay.

That evening, on arriving at Quimper, we pitched up at the depot. Sadly, my friend was not on duty and his deputy didn't hesitate one second before posting us as drivers on the construction line where our two unfortunate comrades had worked. Our morale was in tatters. The following day, just before heading off, I came across my old friend the *chef de feuille* and invited him for a coffee to celebrate the reunion. I told him about the trials of our two colleagues and shared our anxiety with him.

'Don't worry,' he answered, 'that sort of thing doesn't happen every day. What's more, the German railwaymen will be watching out for you. They've got their orders to make sure you're not bothered by the Gestapo. If anything goes amiss, telephone me.'

We were relieved by his words when we set off for Pont l'Abbé. On arrival the station master gave us our instructions.

'Get the bus for Plonéour. The conductor will tell you when to get off. You'll see the works engine and sort things out with the crew you're replacing. But before anything, take these tins of sardines and bully beef. You'll find some cider there already. Unfortunately, I can't give you any bread because all the bakeries are closed. German orders. Punishment for the population on account of the sabotage.'

Just as he had said, the conductor stopped the bus just outside Plonéour.

'This is your stop,' she said.

In the distance we saw a plume of smoke and then the engine of a ballast train coming towards us. As it got closer I recognised the two men in the cab. It was a crew from Bressuire.

'Hey! The relief crew!' shouted the driver. 'Climb aboard, you're taking over at midday.'

We steamed into Reguennec. The Atlantic stretched out as far as the eye could see. The *Pointe du Raz* was on our right, the Eckmuhl lighthouse on the left and America dead ahead.

The Germans were taking thousands of tons of sand from

this huge beach, which they then transferred to different points on the Brittany coast to build their Atlantic Wall. The Bressuire men took us to our new lodgings. These were in a passenger coach with the compartments stripped out. In one corner there was a coal fired stove, a table with some crockery and a few chairs. Two straw mattresses passed for beds. We couldn't complain, given the circumstances. Before taking their leave, our two comrades gave us some bread and said: 'As for the rest, you'll have to do the best you can. Try and pick up something in the countryside. The Bretons are a brave lot but a bit suspicious.'

After an eight-hour shift and a light lunch we set out on a hunt for food. A man from *exploitation* pointed out a farm some two hundred metres from our coach. It had a traditional front, decorated with a cross. When we knocked, an old woman came to the door. We introduced ourselves and explained what we wanted. We quickly found out that we were wasting our time since she spoke only Breton and didn't understand a word of French. When she spoke we hadn't a clue what she said either. Fortunately a handsome woman of around forty came to our aid. She asked us in perfect French what was the reason for our visit.

'In fact, have you got any food to spare?'

'I can see that you're French and not Germans,' she said, 'so in that case, I'll see.'

At that moment her husband appeared. He too was a good looking fellow, finely dressed with a greenish jacket. He was wearing the traditional Breton hat decked with ribbons. His warm face radiated kindness. He took off his hat and jacket and turned towards us.

'Have a seat. What brings you to this part of the world.'

'We work on the railways,' I answered. 'Unfortunately we're not here on a pleasure trip. The Germans sent us.'

'I understand. But where are you from?'

'Near Bordeaux.'

'Ah Bordeaux. That's a big place.'

He appeared surprised that we'd come from so far away.

'I see that you've been around. I've done some traveling myself you know.'

I was waiting for him to say he'd been around the world but he went on,

'I did my military service in Dreux. I've been to Quimper and Chateaulin several times and even Quimplerlé.'

He'd been around the district all right!

'Well then,' he went on, 'since you're from Bordeaux we'll down a bottle from your part of the world. Get us a bottle of Bordeaux from the cellar my dear. At the back, on the left. It's our best.'

As we drank, he asked us exactly what we needed.

'To be honest, we haven't got anything.'

'In that case,' he said, 'let's get a list together. Butter, eggs, pork. . . Have you got something to cook with?'

'Yes, yes!' I said.

These magic words were music to our ears. He continued with his enchanted list.

'Some chicken and cider. And you'll need some bread. Don't you worry, we've got all this. We're not that badly off here in Brittany. The Germans haven't taken everything. The only thing we're really short of is fuel and light.'

They had no electricity at that time and like everyone else they were rationed to a few bags of coal for the year. In addition to this they had a litre of paraffin a month and a handful of carbide [2] for the lamps. I winked at my partner who caught on at once.

'Excuse us a while,' I said to these kind folk, 'we'll be back in half an hour. You won't be in bed will you?'

---

(2) Calcium carbide was used in rock form, mixed with water to produce acetylene gas. Carbide lamps can still be found today but are used mostly for caving.

'No, no. Never before midnight.'

We came back with four 12 kilo briquettes and half a kilo of carbide. They were bowled over with the cargo.

'You won't get into trouble I hope.'

'Not at all. You know the Germans are like us. They don't care a hoot as long as their trains keep running.'

There was nothing we could do to get them to take any money.

'Come back any time,' they said.

In fact, I'd been a little over generous with the carbide as we only had a small amount each month. As it was impossible for us to be without light in the morning and the evening I telephoned the depot at Quimper to get some more. They couldn't help because they too had run out. All that was left to do was to see the German head of the construction job. He was a young captain, about thirty, who had likely been on the Russian front. I was shown into his office and an interpreter was sent for.

I explained why I had come, trying to be as convincing as possible. However, I was taken aback by the officer who looked me straight in the eye with an impassive face. When he spoke firmly to the interpreter I began to regret my plan. I feared the worst. But the interpreter turned to me and said: 'The captain says to you to take 50 kilos of carbide from the store. He asks to you to sign the form for him.'

I wondered if I'd understood him. However I was given a 50 kilos pack of carbide right enough. My Breton friends at the farm would have enough light for a good while!

Our second stay in the red zone lasted until the Pont l'Abbé-Truguennec line was opened. It was used by an 800 ton sand train headed by two 4-6-0 800s which slogged up a 25% gradient. I was surprised to find myself with my old 4-6-0 803 on which I'd been a dedicated fireman ten years earlier at the Saintes depot. The evening we were due to go home we went round to say goodbye to our good Breton comrades who had done so much for us. We offered them a bag of briquettes and a drum of carbide. In return they gave me a copious supply of food, which would leave my wife and daughter wide-eyed in amazement. In north Gironde we were short of everything except wine and wood for the stove. If the region had been as fertile as the Charente we'd have been able to get food, but it wasn't. Still, it must be said that in '43 and '44 some animals were slaughtered clandestinely in the pine forests at night. The women would go out to look for meat under cover of darkness since the sector was teeming with Germans, who came down heavily on this slaughter at their expense.

As I said, we had wine to spare and since the train crews were rightly classed as manual workers, they had the right to a litre a day over and above their monthly rations. What's more, all the wine was transported by rail and I have to tell you a couple of good stories which show just how funny life could be sometimes during the occupation.

Everyone knows the famous expression that it was wine that was the key to the French victory in 1918. I don't know whether this was true or not but the Germans certainly must have thought so in the Second War because they earmarked all the best wines from the Gironde for those serving at the Russian Front. The tanker wagons were constantly being filled in the stations at Coutras, Jonzac, Libourne, Blaye and Saint André de Cubzac. The railwaymen in *traction* and *exploitation* were continually armed with empty bottles, jerry cans and goatskins and even water canteens to fill up when the opportunity presented itself. Some even carried gimlets or small hand drills with small wooden plugs to re-plug the barrels after they'd served themselves.

A large wine depot had been set up at Jonzac station where thousands of litres of red and white wine were dispatched. The head of the depot 'authorised' the railwaymen to help themselves on the side. As the men working in the store refused categorically to take any money we'd pay them in the form of coal, usually briquettes. These briquettes, of course, belonged to the Germans as did the wine, so in fact everything stayed in the family. Some even went as far as saying these were acts of resistance!

Every time we passed Jonzac station on the way to Saintes

we'd fill up our casks. I shared my booty with my parents and in laws. I can say without a word of a lie that I was always well received by the family.

One day I was came into Lapouyarde station working a shunting engine. I had to couple up tanker wagons which were being filled up at the cooperative wine cellar. The train was then to head for Germany. One of the workers gave us a shout.' Come and fill up. It's good stuff, 12⁰ and meant to give the Germans morale a boost on the Russian Front.'

'That's a pity – we just filled up our bottles at the last station.'

But I wasn't beaten yet. I went in to see the *chef de gare*, who was in fact a woman at that time.

'You couldn't lend us some containers, could you?' I asked.

'I've nothing empty unfortunately, only the laundry tub. But it's really big.'

That doesn't matter, in fact so much the better. Let's have it. In a few seconds the vast tub was brimming. My partner grabbed a handle and I took the other. We then carted out the precious liquid, making sure that not a drop was spilt. We then poured it in a half cask which we kept for emergencies. 'Staying ahead means thinking ahead,' I told my partner.

But everyone knows that greed never pays. I was once working with a man called Piol, who was an excellent foreman and the leading actor in an incredible story. It took place at Grave-d'Ambroise station on the Bordeaux-Saintes line. Some think this is a tall story but I give you my word it's true.

The station concerned is about 15 kilometres from the capital of the Gironde and had two wine stores, both with enormous tanks holding thousands of hectolitres. Some were housed underground but other were simply walled in with access taps for emptying. Whenever we were working in the sector we never missed a chance of visiting the 'pissing wall.' The finest Pomerol red wine was destined for our poor wives, to add colour to their cheeks and bolster their red globules in this time of penury.

One day we were running slightly late but, nevertheless, we decided to pay a visit to one of the tanks.

'Get a move on!' shouted the *chef de gare*.

Piol, the train manager and myself got the message and dashed into the huge store. We plunged from brilliant sunshine into the cool obscurity needed for conserving the wine. However, a tanker wagon had just been filled and the workers had not had the time to replace the airtight lid of the underground tank. Piol, who was always the first when it came to drinking, decided to pass across the top of the tank instead of following the path round it. His eyes had still not adapted to the dark and he didn't see the hole. He dropped out of sight into the red wine. He couldn't stand up since the vat was more than two metres deep and when we got to the hole he was screaming his head off and doing the breast stroke in the pool of plonk. The workers gave us a hand to fish him out of his perilous position. He had brushed with the most beautiful death you could think of – drowning in one of Bordeaux's finest vintages.

If the war was sometimes the origin of comical situations and laughable events, the train crews weren't always living it up. More than others we were at the mercy of strafing, sabotage and bombing. Jonzac and Bédenac were undoubtedly the most dangerous places in the area, given that thousands of tons of munitions were stored near both stations. At Jonzac the Germans had camouflaged their reserves in the famous Heurtebise quarries and it was there that two young heroes, Ruibert and Gatineau, sacrificed their lives to blow it up. The Bédenec munitions dump was far more vulnerable to aerial bombardment since the Germans stored the munitions in the pine forests, but despite repeated attempts, the allies never managed to destroy it.

One day, as were coming into Bédenac station at around six in the evening, we heard that the British had dropped incendiary bombs and both sides of the track were ablaze. It was summer and the resinous trees were burning like matchwood, producing gigantic flames. If the wind had been coming from the west, the fire would have reached the Bénedec munitions dump, but it was blowing in the opposite direction and the fire was getting further and further away.

Despite the decision at Saint Mariens station to hold our train until further orders, I wasn't too keen on waiting. I had a new fireman called Rondillac who I was to work with for several years. I asked him what he thought and then had a word with the *chef de train*.

'That's almost thirty hours we've been out.'

'Yes, I wouldn't mind getting home either.'

'The rail crew says that the fire's only on 150 or 200 metres of the track.

We checked the wagons to see that there was no petrol tankers, straw, hay or livestock and then, by common consent we decided to leave. We'd go through the fire and take the consequences.

The dangerous section was about two or three kilometres from Bédenec station so I got the engine up to 40 kilometres an hour as fast as I could. Suddenly we were faced with a wall of fire at least ten metres high and wreathed in smoke.

'Get down in the corner!' I shouted to my partner. He crouched down on the left of the cabin behind the drain taps, while I took shelter between the regulator and the bulkhead. The heat was terrifying and the atmosphere was so suffocating we could hardly breathe. The seconds ticked by as we passed through the hellish tunnel and each one seemed like an hour. At last we steamed out of the blaze intact and could breathe again.

At Saint Mariens the controller and *chef de gare* were waiting on the platform. They'd been informed by telephone from Bédenac and they weren't there to congratulate us.

'You must be mad! Disobeying orders is a serious offense you know. You're lucky nothing happened to the train.'

Clearly they were right. We'd been overkeen to get home and had, without doubt, risked our lives. If I was faced with the same situation now I wouldn't do it – but danger is seen differently through the eyes of a young man.

I was posted three more times at Pont l'Abbé in 1943. The Treguennec line, opened a year earlier, was now fully operational. The trains ran day and night. They passed under a chute which filled up the wagons with sand. It took roughly an hour and a half to load 800 tons and a dozen trainloads ran every twenty four hours using a double header to Pont l'Abbé. From there they were split up and sent to different parts of the Atlantic front.

We were not now billeted on the coast but in Pont l'Abbé, where we were lodged in a large empty house. We had a coal-burning stove, gas, pots and pans and plates – but nothing to put in them. With no canteen to get our meals the only solution was to try and pick up something on the black market in the countryside. Since we could no longer visit our farmhouse friends, we perfected a new system. When I was driving back empty for reloading I slowed down in front of a farm we'd been told about so that the fireman could jump off and I'd carry on alone. A couple of hours later, passing the same spot with a load of sand, I'd pick up my partner. We then tossed out some briquettes in the ditch in exchange for the food the Bretons gave us.

I can tell you that all the train crews who were working away from home and from whatever depot did the same, simply because it was the only way to get food. The railway police didn't take our methods kindly but what was unacceptable in peace time appeared legitimate under the yoke of the occupation. Moreover the Germans were perfectly aware of this, but all they wanted was for their sand trains to keep running and so turned a blind eye on the matter.

Of course you didn't have to abuse the system. One day a crew from I depot I won't name, exchanged an entire pig for a tender of coal. To carry the payment away the peasants had to come with wagons pulled by oxen. If the engine had left on time, nothing would have come out, but the tender, which everyone had seen full the day before, had to be refilled on the side by shovel. The police got onto it and arrested the two men. They were only released on orders from the Germans who gave the following extenuating circumstances: 'These men had no canteen and so they had to make out as best as they could.'

A service notice was put up the same day on the door of our lodgings by the occupying army.

NOTICE
Any SNCF employee provoking late running of sand trains will be deported to Germany to work.

The notice made us take more care, but the secret food procurement continued until the Americans arrived.

I never understood why the Allies didn't bomb the Treguennec installations, the silos and the loading chutes. Every night the sirens went up, the lights went out and we heard the roar of the aircraft above us. But not a single bomb was dropped and the work was never interrupted.

It was a different story at Cherbourg. In December 1943 I was posted away from home for three weeks in this highly dangerous sector. I'd rather have gone back to Pont l'Abbé, but orders were orders. After passing through Paris we came to Volognes where the Germans went through the train from top to bottom. You had to be squeaky clean to get into a red zone. We weren't troubled since we were actually working for them.

This was my first visit to Cherbourg and a sorry sight it was to see. During our three week posting the famous Cherbourg drizzle never stopped for a minute but when it eased up, it was the bombs that started to rain down.

Our train had barely pulled in when the sirens started to wail. I reached the shelter with my partner and the relentless bombardment lasted half an hour. The British target was the Roule mountain, just above the SNCF loco depot where hundreds of men from the occupied countries had been forced to work by the Germans. The explosions caused numerous victims among these unfortunate souls who were sacrificed without a second thought. A few hours after the attack we saw trucks packed with dead bodies roll into Cherbourg with blood flowing from cracks in the slatted sides.

The service was far more varied than at Pont l'Abbé. We worked in the Ocean Terminal and sometimes took locomotives to Lison for maintenance. Then again at times we got engines ready or replaced train crews. Quite often we hauled wagons to the Gottefast and Martinvast stations, where

German railwaymen would take over to run the trains into the mysterious complex where foreigners were not allowed to enter. One day I decided to ask one of them why we weren't allowed in. He answered in a pathetic voice and without a smile: 'That's where they are constructing the most terrible weapon that will destroy England.'

Perhaps he was alluding to the V1 and V2 rockets, the horrific weapons which were to ravage the civilian population the following year.

After three weeks of air raid warnings and incessant air attacks we returned to Saint Mariens for New Year's Day 1944, hoping to find some respite. But our hopes were in vain. The day after I got home, at around one in the morning, my wife and I were woken up suddenly by a violent explosion which clearly came from the depot. The resistance had just blown up eight slide valves and eight high-pressure cylinders on some 4-6-0 locos which were parked on the exit line some 300 metres from where we lived. My 4-6-0 number 045 was one of them.

The explosions stirred up plenty of trouble. The German soldiers swarmed into the depot and were quickly joined by the Gestapo from Bordeaux. At the same time rumours started circulating that hostages would be taken. The mayor gave himself up in a bid to avoid the population being affected. The Germans stopped all trains for the French apart from worker trains to Bordeaux which provided them with an indispensable labour force. They also took some engines that were unscathed for their own use. Throughout the rest of the night, the Gestapo interrogated the *chef de reserve* and those having access to the depot. Two days after they imprisoned the depot watchman. This was not because they thought that he was to blame, but because he refused to say what he had seen. After the Liberation we learnt that the sabotage had been carried out by two railwaymen from *operations*. The attack had been perfectly organised by the two members of the *Résistance Fer.* [3]

In the meantime the damaged engines were sent to the Saintes workshops where they were fitted with new cylinders and three weeks later they were fixed and back again. After

---

(3) This was the name given to the railway resistance group.

several months in prison the depot watchman was given a conditional release thanks to the German railwaymen's intervention. The outcome of the attack was tighter surveillance and harassment of train crews. At night the depot was guarded by the army. On arrival when we were about 100 metres from the gate, the sentry would shout out, 'Halt!' and then, in the pitch black, he would come and check us. Once he knew that we were '*machinistes*' as they called us, we were let through. But a soldier armed with a machine gun followed us like a shadow when we went to our lockers to get changed or when we were getting oil or greasing the engine. After several days, without discussing the matter, we ended up knowing each other. The atmosphere eased and the older Germans watched us less keenly. When the Gestapo got to know of this they ordered the army to change our surveillants every eight days. These watch dogs didn't leave us until June 1944 when they were needed to fight on the Normandy Front.

Before coming round to the Allied landings and the great moments of the Resistance on the railways, I have to say something about one of the German railwaymen who was in charge of us throughout the entire occupation. I've already had the opportunity to show that they were more understanding than the army and sometimes managed to get us out of extremely tight situations.

At Saint Mariens the German head was in *traction* and was the *chef de reserve* in the Frankfurt region, not far from the French frontier. He spoke French perfectly and was open in his views with some of us, except when there were other Germans around, even railwaymen. I remember his reaction when the Americans entered the war.

'So much the better,' he said, to my face, 'it may shorten the war, because now there's no way Germany can win.'

He had understood for a long time what would be the outcome of the conflict.

'I'm not that bothered about the great German Reich and the New Order,' he'd often say to us. 'I prefer a little Reich and to be near my wife and kids.'

Once I was enjoying my rest day working in the garden in

brilliant sunshine when I saw him walk by. He was on his daily visit to the depot to call on his counterpart, the French *chef de reserve*. He stopped to watch me work. We started to talk about nothing in particular.

'Come and have a glass of white with me,' he said. suddenly,' nodding towards a small café which was run by an old lady.

'No,' I replied, 'I can't.'

He looked at me with sadness in his eyes and said: 'I understand. You don't want to drink with a *Boche*, do you?'

'You have to understand,' I said in a friendly tone. 'It's risky to drink with somebody who's occupying your country. It's different for you. In our eyes, you're just a railwayman. You don't wear a uniform and you're not here for fun. You don't hate the French. On the contrary. But you have to see it's not a good time for us to be seen drinking together in a *bistro*. I might be suspected of collaboration.'

He went off, his head hung low.

But half an hour later he was back, with a bottle wrapped up in a newspaper.

'I've just bought a fine bottle. We could hide up somewhere and share it. I'd like that, wouldn't you? Come on, nobody's going to see.'

He looked at me pleadingly. How can you resist such a human gesture?

'Go to the pine copse in front of the stadium,' I said to him, 'so we won't be seen going together. I'll join you there.'

Hidden behind the trees, we drank the bottle with a glass I'd brought. He told me about his wife and children. I could see he was glad to be with a friend. How sad and stupid war is. An apt expression came to me: 'War involves a lot of men killing men who they don't even know for the benefit of a few other men who know each other and never get killed at all.'

I didn't feel as if I was collaborating. I was simply glad to share a glass with a decent fellow.

The damage at Chambéry in 1944 shows why the
Germans avoided activity in large depots
(La Vie du Rail)

A pair of 2-8-2s test the improvised repairs
on the Canardièe viaduct near Chantilly
(La Vie du Rail)

Chapter 8
Liberation

ON 6 JUNE 1944 just as I was coming on shift at the
Saint Mariens depot, I heard a points man say that the
Americans had landed on the Normandy coast. There had been
so many empty rumours about this, that I remained sceptical,
but I found out that it was true when I arrived at Saintes with
the goods train I was heading. It was the beginning of the end
for the Germans. That evening I slept at my parents', at Saint
Eutrope. Their house was a long way from the station and
consequently less exposed to air raids. The next day I was back
at Saint Mariens and took a rest day after seven on duty.

For hundreds of thousands of men, women and children,
the 6th June was the longest day. As for me, it was the night of
the 8th to the 9th that was the longest and one I'll never
forget. On the 8th, at around 7 in the evening the *inspecteur
d'exploitation* arrived at the depot along with some German
railwaymen and soldiers. The latter demanded two engines and
two train crews immediately to go for a German train waiting
at Saint-Médard-de-Guiziéres, a station just beyond Coutras. It
was carrying troops who had been pulled back from the
Périgord maquis to reinforce the Normandy Front. The *chef de
réserve* told them that it wouldn't be easy to find two crews at
that time but after much to-ing and fro-ing he had to give in.
As I was living near the depot he picked me to go. On arrival
at the office I did everything I could to avoid the duty – and
my bosses did their best to help.

'That's not possible,' they said, 'these men are on their rest
day.' It was then that a German officer stepped in with a curt,
'You will send two *machines* and two crews. Departure 8
o'clock. That is an order.'

There was nothing left to do but carry it out. Five of us left for Coutras. There was Rondillac and myself, the other crew and a man from *operations*.

It may seem strange that this troop of soldiers should be held at tiny Saint Médard-de-Guiziéres, but that was in line with a general order from the German high command. Locomotive changes had to take place at small stations because all the big depots and marshalling yards had been systematically strafed and bombed by the Allies.

It was pitch black when we arrived at Coutras.

'The Allies are drubbing Poitiers now,' shouted the station master. 'The station and the depot. Don't hang about. We could be next.'

Although the power was cut, we first had to turn the engines around as there was no question of running to Saintes tender first. No sooner requested than the order was given and twenty Germans turned up to man the turntable by hand. We took advantage of the time to get something to eat by lamplight at the guard room, as we'd had nothing since midday.

At Saint Médard, we coupled up the passenger train full of young soldiers, who appeared to be delighted to go to battle in Normandy. They had been bored in the *maquis* [1] where pitched battles had been few and far between. We left at 11.30 on the up line and arrived at Coutras minutes later. We didn't stay there long.

'They've reached Angouleme!' warned the assistant station master. 'They're getting nearer and could be here any time. Take water at Saint Mariens as fast as you can and get the hell out of here.' We didn't need a second telling.

The two engines were signalled to stop at Saint Mariens on the main line. While the tender was being watered some madman came out of the leading coach, which carried the officers, and came up to me.

'*Monsieur*!' he began, 'You will leave at once. We are going to battle.'

---

(1) The Limousin, central France. Also used for the Resistance.

I nodded at the stop signal. He then started to scream.

'I told you to leave at once. That is an order!'

The maniac climbed into the cab, pulled out his pistol and shoved it against my ribs.

'At once! Leave at once!'

'Alright, alright, just calm down.'

Luckily, Rondillac noticed that the German railwaymen's boss – a white wine expert by the way – was standing next to the train. Rondillac ran up to him to explain what had happened. Our German colleague arrived, took the pistol from the raging officer and gave him such a dressing down that he shut up there and then and sloped off back to his carriage. The German railwayman then turned to us: 'The poor dimwit can't wait to get killed.'

Minutes later we were steaming towards Saintes. The leading engine made the pace. As second locomotive I was there simply to back her up. Suddenly, as we were running down a 10% grade just after Fontaines-Ozillac, the leading driver slammed on the brakes. I had seen nothing on account of the blackness and the engine in front which blocked my view of the road. Neither had I heard any detonators. But I was sure that something was wrong. I could do nothing to brake more quickly and simply opened the sand valve to help the grip. Luckily the German troop trains had virtually all the coaches braked and they could pull up in four or five hundred metres. Ahead a red lantern indicated a mandatory stop. It was the middle of the night, yet there was bustle all around. German soldiers and railwaymen along with the Jonzac station staff, scurried about. We very soon realised why they were there: the railway bridge on the Bordeaux-Saintes line, which linked it to a small branch line, had been blown up.

When the Resistance had heard that our train was carrying troops to the Normandy Front, they had done everything they could to sabotage the bridge. They'd probably threatened the line-safety manager, forcing him not to put detonators on the track and told him to leave the signal at Montendre, a few kilometres before the bridge, open. For them, it was clearly a case for conscience: sacrifice five railwaymen – four from *traction* and one from *operations* – to accomplish a blow for France. A cruel dilemma.

Fortunately the leading driver had seen something in the distance. It was the red lamp which the Germans had rigged. Consequently he'd been able to stop in time. His reflex had been all the more remarkable since there was nothing else to warn us of the danger. If he hadn't been wide awake, we'd have all perished in the derailment. Our wives would have become widows and we would have become heroes. Our names would have been carved on the marble plaque, in the hall of Saint-Mariens station, of those lost in the war. And then, every year on the 11th of November, flowers would be duly placed and a speech given. It's not that the Resistance was wrong, but on that day Providence was against them, and perhaps that wasn't such a bad thing.

Already the line men were at work. It took them an hour and a half to replace the two main timbers that supported the track, then to lay two lengths of rail. The train could then pass over at 6 kilometres an hour. The officers were livid at the delay and from then on saw 'terrorists' everywhere. They posted armed guards in the two cabs, ordering to shoot any *maquisards* they saw next to the line. The time passed slowly, I can tell you, what with the barrels of the machine guns rubbing against our backsides. We saw nobody, thank Heavens, because I'm sure in the state they were in, our guardians would have shot anyone on sight, even the most innocent bystander. At last, dawn broke and we changed engines at Beillant, a tiny station chosen by the Germans because it had been targeted less than Saintes. We breathed a deep sigh of relief as we watched the train head north. The next stop would be the end of the line for them in more ways than one.

The greatest moment for the Resistance was undoubtedly the summer of 1944. Just after the Normandy landings their actions took on a new dimension. It's difficult to write anything new on this, given all the books covering the subject and René Clement's film *La Bataille du Rail*. I'd just like to show, using my own modest experiences, that things were not so black and white and that it was very difficult to counter the

Nazis without risking the lives of fellow countrymen at the same time.

There were a good many railwaymen in the Resistance, all playing different roles. The train crews were the best placed to sabotage material, but also the most exposed to reprisals by the Germans, who punished any hint of sabotage severely. At best it was deportation and at worst the firing squad. Some examples taken before the Allied landings show how tricky our situation was.

One day I was in Guitres station, which was not far from Coutras. I had a few minutes in hand before taking a goods train and I used them to grease the valve gear and the wheels on the tender. This meant a few less jobs to do the next morning at Saint Mariens. The assistant station master came up to me.

'Did you hear the British on the radio last night?'

'Yes.'

'Then why are you greasing the engine?'

True, the British broadcaster had said: 'Railwaymen! Sabotage your engines! Resist the Occupation!'

Easily said from a studio, but those who advise are not necessarily those who pay. It was true that we worked for the Germans, but we also helped to get food for the French. Sabotaging our engines meant starving our families. I understood the man, who was a good friend. He was sincere in his convictions and a *Résistant* to the core. But his situation was not the same as mine.

Some days after this I was heading the regular works train from Saint Mariens to Coutras. I had 600 tons behind and that meant a full load. When we got to Guitres the same assistant station master came up.

'Fifty tons more lads! Two tanks of red.'

(La Vie du Rail) A Vichy poster shows the classic sabotage of destroying the cylinders and warns the French of the consequences.

SABOTAGE YOUR ENGINES? SABOTAGE SUPPLIES! WHO CAN PROTECT THE LOCOMOTIVES AND THE LIVES OF YOUR COMRADES? YOU, THE RAILWAYMAN

Evidence shows that the argument was true and that the Germans prioritised locos for troop transport and work trains

'Sorry,' retorted the guard, 'we've a full load. We can't take any more.'

'It's an order from *exploitation*, said the assistant. These wagons are for Germany.'

'I refuse to take them,' insisted the guard, sticking to the regulations. 'If you want you can ask the driver if he'll take the extra load.'

I gave exactly the same reply.

'Come on! Surely you can take the extra 50 tons.'

'Of course I could take them and I'd make it up the grade because my engine's a worker and not a shirker. But this extra load's for the Germans and so there's no question of doing it.'

'Very well.'

He then uncoupled the last two wagons carrying food for the French and had the two tanks for the Germans take their place. This prompted me to give him a short lesson in consistency.

'Just the other day,' I began, 'you were at me for greasing my engine, saying that I was disobeying our orders from London. But what you've just done is more serious. You're sacrificing food for the French and replacing it with drink for the Germans. I'd call that collaboration.'

'I've got nothing to do with this. They're orders from the Germans. I don't want any trouble.'

'You see!' I concluded, 'It's easy to be in the Resitance if you don't take risks.'

He didn't say another word, but he'd understood. He's never mentioned the matter since.

The Central Service Inspector, an expert in braking systems and a man who stuck to principles, was an entirely different kettle of fish. He'd often accompany us to make sure that nobody bent the rules. He was with me once in Coutras station when a problem came up. The needle on the brake pressure gauge was not budging, even though the pump was in perfect order.

'Check the train,' he said.

We weren't long in finding the guilty connecting hose. It had been slashed with a knife, in the name of the Resistance of course.

'Take a look at that,' he said. 'That's the work of idiots. It's not worth a thing. The Germans won't be pushed back because of that. All it does is annoy them. It makes them more suspicious, that's all. There'll be a time when you'll be asked to make your contribution to the Resistance – when the time is right. But for God's sake, none of this personal initiative stuff. We should all work together.'

After the war we discovered that the inspector was in fact the head of *Resistance Fer*.

Not long after the endless night of the 8th to the 9th June I was again rostered on a troop train for Normandy. We had two engines from Saint Mariens to replace the two bringing the train from Bordeaux and then run as far as Marans, just north of Rochelle. At that time the British were strafing locomotives all the time. Consequently we weren't exactly overkeen to leave.

When the train from Bordeaux steamed in around nine in the morning we claimed that our engines were damaged. The head of the German railwaymen turned a blind eye to our delaying tactics but the officers in charge of the troop train realised what was going on and telephoned Saintes, asking for measures to be taken. Our German railway colleague immediately sought us out.

'Get this train out of here as fast as you can otherwise you'll be in serious trouble,' he said. 'A car's on its way to Saintes. You can do what you want on the way, but for the moment, for God's sake, just get the train moving.'

It was best to take his advice, settle for a six hour delay and head for Rochelle. I drove second, since my engine was actually badly damaged.

The brakes on the locomotive and the rolling stock worked on compressed air. The pump, situated on the front of the engine compressed the air and sent it into the primary and secondary reservoirs and from there through the system. However, I had two kilos of air pressure when five were needed to service the train. I knew perfectly well what lay behind the failure. It was a very clever piece of sabotage. In order to maintain a perfect seal on the two cylinders in the pump and the rod, they were lined with a special ant-friction alloy. In the workshops, the workers in the Resistance had found out that by altering the proportions of lead and antimony of the alloy, it lost some of its anti-friction qualities. Consequently, the lead would partly melt provoking cracks in the lining and so producing a leak in the airtightness. And so the pump, which appeared to be working normally, could not supply the system with the pressure needed for the brakes. It goes without saying that it took an expert to see through it.

When we got to Saintes we asked for a relief crew from *traction* but there was no question of it. The Germans found that we had already lost enough time and ordered us to set off for Marans once we'd taken water. All went fine until Rochelle, but on pulling into the station the bars on the leading engine started to collapse. The ash had not been cleaned out for days and the air was not getting through. Consequently the bars were red hot and were starting to melt thus forcing my colleague to an emergency dash for the depot to drop the fire. The leading machine was now out of commission and the haggling started.

So there we were, my partner and I, alone at the head of the train, reduced to waiting for a replacement loco from the réserve depot at Rochelle. The German officers quickly got impatient as usual. With their incessant mania for attacking the drivers, rather than going to the operating staff, they approached me and asked in a threatening tone why I wasn't leaving.

'Engine failure,' I replied. 'We're waiting for a second loco because this one isn't strong enough to haul the train.'

It's extremely difficult to make yourself understood with people who can't understand French and who know absolutely nothing about railways. They took to screaming like savages with the word sabotage often cropping up in their tirades. Fortunately the racket was noticed by the German railway staff who came up to me and politely asked what was the problem. I showed them the air pressure gauge at 2 kilos.

They finally made the German officers see reason and they went back to their coach. In fact the German Railway managers were in charge of the stations, depots and anything to do with the railways. They reckoned that my engine wasn't in sufficiently good condition to work a train. I was sent to the Rochefort depot and they telephoned for another loco to be sent from Rochelle. This was another occasion where the French railwaymen were helped out of trouble by our German counterparts.

The day ended on a dramatic note. We heard by telephone that the two engines sent from Rochelle had been strafed at Saint Laurent de la Prée station. The troop train, therefore, wasn't going to leave Rochefort for a while yet.

That evening, arriving back at Saintes, I couldn't stop thinking about the worker in the Resistance who had sabotaged my pump. I saw him as a father with an easy conscience, always seemingly harmless, filing away at his work bench. His actions perhaps would put him up for a decoration after the war. Undoubtedly he did it in the name of the Resistance but in doing so he put others at risk. He took the crown of laurels all right, but left the train crews with the one of thorns.

From June to August 1944 it was chaos on the railways. The trains were never on time and sometimes they never even got to their destination. The Resistance were forever sabotaging locomotives and blowing up the track.

The Germans realised that it was the end. In Normandy the Americans, not worrying about details, executed some German railwaymen on the spot. The international rules of war deemed that anyone not wearing a uniform could be judged as a sniper and so could be executed without trial. The German high command therefore, made the railwaymen wear army uniforms in order to counter this. They had been so full of themselves after their *Blitzkrieg* that they had overlooked the need for such a useful precaution. But the change of clothes did nothing to bolster the German railwaymen's morale. I heard that in Bordeaux they smashed their rifles on the engine buffers as a measure of their despair.

The air raids on the stations and depots worsened by the day. You couldn't even count the number of engines out of action from strafing. In early July I was almost another one of their victims when the tender and boiler of the engine I was working was riddled with bullets just seconds after we'd run for cover.

It was in these kind of conditions that I was ordered one day to head an empty train from Saintes to Bordeaux with a works loco. After my rest day at Saintes I found the engine in question in a sorry state. There wasn't a drop of oil in the lubricator and only one of the injectors was working. But orders were orders and I slowly headed south. At Saint Mariens my wife gave me a wave from the house and I signalled to her that I was pressing on for Bordeaux. When I finally reached the destination the engine was uncoupled and sent to the depot.

I was at the entry to the depot preparing to take on coal when the assitant head came up and asked: 'What state's this engine in?'

'Not so good.'

'You can handle it as you want, but this engine mustn't leave. The Germans are waiting for it. At the moment there are several troop trains for Normandy stranded for want of locomotives. When the Germans come, tell them the engine's damaged. Understand. Orders from the Resistance.'

So I was to sabotage the job. But it wasn't as simple as that. Then I had the idea of neutralising the second injector to stop the feed to the boiler completely. The Germans were swarming all over the depot and prudence was the watchword. To make matters worse, both railwaymen and soldiers now had the same uniform. I climbed on the boiler casually and with my adjustable tightened the needle that governed the inlet valve. I'd just got down when two Germans shouted over to me.

'Get coal on; get water on. Quickly. *Machine* leaves straight away.'

'*Machine kaput.*' I said.

My reply had the effect of sending them into a rage.

'*Machine* always *kaput!* It is sabotage.'

In a bid to calm them down I showed them that both injectors were damaged.

'Impossible to move. Impossible.' I added.

'Bring worker. Right away!' they shouted.

The technician duly arrived and began to nose around the injectors. If he looked closely there was a good chance that he'd detect the sabotage. The Germans followed his every move.

'This doesn't look too good,' I said to my partner. 'Let's get out of here.'

We picked up our bags and covers from the tender and drifted behind the engine where we couldn't be seen. We then sprinted off towards the passenger station. According to the book we should have clocked out at the depot office but the Germans could have tracked us down. Consequently, I decided to go through the station and then cross the railway bridge and seek relative safety in Benauge station.

'Any trains to Saint Mariens,' I asked the assistant *chef de service* when we arrived at Benauge.

'Nothing for the moment. All passenger trains have been cancelled except the works train at half past seven. But you never know, there may be a train or an engine going through this afternoon.'

'Well, we've nothing to do for the present and nothing to eat either.'

I nodded in the direction of a nearby bistro. 'Let's go for a drink,' I said to my partner.

'Good thinking,' he replied.

We were welcomed by a handsome woman, around forty who seemed to recognise me.

'What brings you here then? Don't you remember me?'

'I do now! You used to run a café at Royan.'

'That's right! I've been in Benauge for a while now. Things are going alright and I can't complain. My, I'm glad to see you. It brings back good memories of Royan. Here, let me give you a kiss on the cheek!'

'Go ahead!'

We told her of our close shave, then the conversation shifted on the great age of Royan and all the things that we'd been through together. When she invited us for lunch we accepted whole heartedly and I have to say we never regretted our acceptance. Right in the middle of August, after years of rationing it was a real feast that awaited us. I rediscovered the taste of things that had practically disappeared because of the war: olive oil in a tomato salad, cucumber and spices, a thick slice of ham with chips, creamy cheese that had nothing to do with the tasteless stuff we'd grown used to. And then there was the coffee and glass of cognac.

'I had quite a few German customers,' she explained. 'They saw me right for food – for them of course – but now you can reap the benefit.'

She'd wouldn't accept payment although we tried our hardest. In the meanwhile, the assistant at the station had managed to arrange for our departure.

When we were back at the station he announced: 'There's an empty due at around three. It's not supposed to stop but I'll drop the stop signal and you can climb on.'

We were back in Saint Mariens by four.

Since I lived between the station and the depot, life became tiresome. We were continually being called out and every night we had to wake up our little six year old daughter to take shelter in the woods nearby. Therefore I gladly accepted the offer of the station master at Saint Savin de Blaye, a small village set amongs vineyards and some 5 kilometres from Saint Mariens.

'Tell Madame Péroche to come too, with the little one. She can stay in the station. It's quiet here, there's nothing to

bomb.' We moved at the end of July and stayed until
September.

We could sense that Liberation was coming, and now we
set about systematic sabotage in order to put the whole railway
out of commission. Nevertheless, in the final weeks of fighting
in the west of France, the railwaymen still had a heavy price to
pay. It was one morning that I learnt with a heavy heart that a
fireman who had worked with me in Syria had been killed.
This fine friend was always saying: 'If I see a plane coming at
us I'll be flat out on the coal in the tender no mistake.'

The previous evening, when he'd been driving a works
train back from Bordeaux, his 2-4-0 had been straffed by a
British fighter. It must have been obvious that it was an old
engine and the train could only have been carrying French
passengers but at that time the Allies didn't make distinctions.
My comrade carried out his survival plan. He'd thrown himself
on the tender and recieved several bullets through his head. In
a terrible case of irony, the enquiry showed that if he hadn't
moved, he'd have survived. At his funeral the whole of Saint
Mariens was in tears. The driver was badly wounded, but
recovered after several months in hospital.

Right up until the end the Germans reigned our area with
terror. For instance, when they were passing by the little
station of Saint-Savin, they fired at the walls of our lodgings.
We were terrified but nobody was hit. After this show of
gratuitous violence they fired on a group of so called
maquisards carrying only knapsacks. In their retreat the
Germans also carried out systematic destruction of the railways
with the aim of paralysing the network, which they knew
would be needed by the Allies. They blew up vital links such as
the Beillant bridge over the Charente and the Saint-André-de-
Cubzac bridge over the Dordogne, one of Eiffel's masterpieces.

After sabotaging our equipment to hamper the enemy we
had to turn to the task of rebuilding what had been destroyed
in the fighting. The soil of our homeland had still not yet been
totally liberated. Heavy fighting continued in the east and the
Charente coast was still occupied. We had to help the Allies to
retake Royan and Rochelle and get food to the civilians. The
most difficult problem about getting any kind of regular

service was crossing the rivers after the bridges had been dynamited. It would take months for these to be rebuilt by civil engineers. In the meantime the trains from Saintes were diverted to Beillant where the coaches crosssed the Charente on the road bridge. Since the bridge was not strong enough to take the 120 or so tons of locomotive, another engine from the Saint Mariens depot waited on the other side to take the train south.

This diversion involved substantial works. The SNCF called on all the diffferent services with the exception, of course of the train crews, the safety men and the pointsmen, who had to remain at their posts. All the railway staff, white collar workers included, took up pick and shovel and put their shoulders to the wheel. They showed that after being involved in the liberation of their country they were ready to participate in the reconstruction. At the same time, others were going ahead with clearing up the damage at Saintes station and getting it back into service. The depot workers too weren't unemployed. What with the scanty maintenance, sabotage, accidents and the strafed engines they put in months of tireless effort to repair the locomotives.

The second problem on the Bordeaux line was the river Dordogne. The Saint-André bridge had also been blown up. At first, the passengers were ferried across before rejoining another train to Bordeaux. But this could only be a temporary solution and so all the traffic was branched off onto the Libourne line and from there onto the electrified Paris-Bordeaux line. It was vital to speed up the goods trains, since rationing was biting hard, even more than during the occupation. Up to the liberation the Germans had taken the cake but had left us the crumbs. Now, nothing was being distributed. It wasn't a handful of trucks running on gas generators that were going to solve the problem. It was clear to everyone that the railways should be number one priority.

Little by little the trains restarted from Chateauneuf, Blaye, Coutras and Libourne. A special engine and wagon was commissioned to distribute flour to the bakers in the Saint Mariens district using a central flour mill at Barbezieux in Charente. The slaughter houses also were back at work and the situation for our families gradually got better. And then there was our new found freedom, which made us forget our hunger.

At the end of summer 1944, as if the war hadn't claimed enough victims, I risked a terrible death out of sheer professional pride. It would be dishonest to skip over this offense, for which I was totally responsible. The Germans had just pulled out of the area when the PC sent me to Bordeaux with a light train to work an omnibus as far as Beillant. As trains were still a rarity, passenger trains were alwys full to bursting. Therefore a powerful engine was needed. The PC had earmarked a 4-6-0 800 but since I trusted my 4-6-0 065, which I'd been in charge of since coming back from Le Mans, I asked my chief if I could use her. After an initial refusal and a telephone call he said, 'You take responsibility then. I can give you authorisation but watch out. You've got every interest that nothing goes wrong, otherwise you'll pay for it.'

I worked down to Bordeaux where I managed to find some good coal thanks to a litre of fine white for the chute operators. Then it was off again with 450 tons behind – therefore, overloaded. I passed through Saint Mariens feeling full of myself, and gave a wave to the wife, who saw that everything was alright. However, the *chef de réserve,* who was standing in front of his office, didn't look happy.

His anxiety was justified. Just after Jonzac the engine started using water like nobody's business. She was steaming well and there didn't seem to be a leak and yet we had everything to do to keep her in water. At Pons the water was on the bottom rim of the glass and we still had 14 kilometres to go. I took advantage of the two minute halt to jump onto the front buffers and open the smoke box. The autoclaver was leaking badly which meant it had either come loose or the seal had gone. My heart sank.

'It's God's punishment!'

We just managed to limp into Beillart where a driver who was standing in for the chief barked out: 'Drop the fire. For the return leg there's another a passenger train. Take a 4-6-0 800.'

I was in a right mess. When he got back, my boss would be riding high. I could already hear him: 'He's always wiser than the rest Péroche. He wanted his engine did he? Well he had to take an 800 to get him back.' I was so frightened of wounded pride that I decided to do everything I could to rescue the situation.

'Listen,' I said to the chief's stand in, 'if I could stop the leak, everything would be alright.'

'You're crazy!' he replied. 'There's no question of it.'

And without listening to me further he marched off to give instructions for the 4-6-0 800 to be moved onto the line.

And so it was that despite his instructions, I decided to undertake a highly dangerous repair. I had to crawl into the smoke box where it was around 70^0 and where the carbon monoxide may well suffocate me. If the seal was just loose, then a turn with the adjustable would be all that was needed. If the seal was cracked, however, the same turn could break it and I'd be boiled alive. I could hardly breathe now, with the gas burning my throat, but I managed to get around the exhaust column. The heat was terrible. I was sweating like a pig and my knees were bathed in boiling water. I groped for the seal head and got my adjustable round it. My life depended on what happened next. I tightened it gently The leak didn't stop. Should I go on?

'To hell with it!'

I gave it a full half turn. The leak stopped!

Now, I had to get out of this furnace. I was soaked from head to foot and coughing like the devil. At last I dropped in front of the engine without using the steps and lay down on the earth.

I gradually got my breath back.

'That was a miracle by God,' I said raising my eyes to the Heavens.

Moments later the stand-in chief arrived.

'That's it. The 800's ready.

'She won't be needed. I'll get back with my engine.'

'But look here, that's impossible.'

'The leak's fixed.'

I explained what I'd done. He was livid.

'Do you realise what you've done? What if the seal broke up? You'd be dead and not without suffering. And it would have been me responsible for it.'

My pride was satisfied because I wouldn't be treated like a fool back at Saint-Mariens. But I knew his anger was justified a thousand times over.

'Don't hold it against me. I admit I was wrong, but what's done's done. Let's split the difference over a drink.'

I don't know what got into me that day. I often think about that experience in the smoke box and even today I get the shivers when I think of an end that I would have fully deserved.

The end of 1944. The war is far from over. Heavy fighting is still going on in the east of the country. Large numbers of American ships are docking in Cherbourg and le Havre with hundreds of locomotives and rolling stock destined to take men and materials to the front. The Americans, therefore, are terribly short of train crews and so, naturally, appeal to the French .

Consequently, I'm called to Cherbourg in December, but this time in the camp of the victors. Rondillac, my partner at that time, is posted with me.

It was no small matter just getting to a strategic military port. A special DMU went around picking up rail men from Saint Mariens, Saintes, Niort and Rochelle. At Nantes, the rail bridge was down and we had to make our way to a second train on foot. The train then passed through le Mans, then crossed into the Manche *département*. To reach Cherbourg we passed through towns which had suffered tremendously during the battle of Normandy: Saint Lo, Saint Mere l'Eglise, Valognes.

The air raids had caused extensive damage and the Germans had done the rest. The bridges had been blown, the water columns destroyed and the signals, both electrical and mechanical, had simply disappeared.

At Cherbourg we met the Americans, who had taken over the railways completely. The French railwaymen helped them, but the Americans gave the orders. Their first task was to repair the bridges and get the tracks back in service. They had started vast construction projects to re-establish access to Cherbourg. The Germans had blocked a tunnel by blowing up a munitions train inside it but by working around the clock, the Americans managed to open it and the line was quickly in service again.

There were no signals and so they improvised a system. If a train left Cherbourg for a destination whatsoever, in principle it didn't stop. Only detonaters overode the drivers running by sight. If that happened, then, at the first sheltered point, the driver halted the train and used a lighted torch which acted as a flare. Then he just waited for further orders to arrive.

The sheer extent of the American organisation was remarkable, but our greatest surprise was at the abundance in which they lived. They set up a canteen in each station and fed us, at no charge, a very rich diet. This was made up of tinned and frozen food such as turkey, beef, mushrooms, fruit and pancakes topped with pineapple juice. In short, we lacked for nothing. All this food had added vitamins, so much so that it made you feel a bit strange. The smokers had all the cigarettes they wanted.

Of course they wanted a return on all this. They had absolutely nothing to do with organising the work, even less so than the Germans. For them, everything was always urgent. At Cherbourg the ships unloaded day in, day out and the goods were distributed immediately, so helping to consolidate victory. But unlike with the Germans, we all put our heart in helping the Americans.

Our relations with the American railwaymen were founded on a decision by the Allied high command. 'The French run the trains and American traction managers run the railway.' That meant there was always an American rail man with you in

Opposite (top) The Americans started to stock locomotives in Britain in 1942. This park in Wales shows hundreds of identical 2-8-0s waiting for D-Day

(bottom) Lowering the boiler onto the chassis of a 2-8-0 on arrival at Cherbourg (La Vie du Rail)

the cab to tell you what to do. But it was far more difficult to communicate with them than with our former 'occupants'. A good many Germans spoke French and could at least make out what you were trying to say. With our American friends it was down to sign language. No doubt there were some American rail men who spoke French, but I didn't come across any.

The American rail men were always very generous with us. Once, when I was at a halt at Valognes, I was warming myself in front of the open firebox since I didn't have my working overalls. The American managed to say to me, 'Why you no cover?' I gave the gesture for 'That's life!' He then leapt off the engine, without using the steps and came back with a superb new lumber jacket. They had as many shops as they had canteens. How could people with wealth like that possibly have lost the war?

Another time the American rail man with me saw that my feet were freezing since my shoes were completely worn though and I was stamping to keep my feet warm. At the next station he left and came back with two new pairs of leather boots. He told me to try them on to see which was my size and then he took back the other pair. But what struck the Americans most was that we didn't wear gloves since they wore them all the time. They gave me several pairs but I was so used to working bare-handed I never used them.

The American's overriding principle was never to economise. The steam locomotives that they brought over were immensely powerful and very up to date but not made to last. They used vast quantities of oil and were greedy on coal. Whenever there was a derailment – in a station or on the open track – they simply lifted the engine off the track and replaced it with a new one.

'No time to repair it buddy,' they used to say. 'The French can do it after the war.'

And, in fact, that's what happened. In 1945 they gave a good many locomotives to the SNCF.

During the night of 23rd to the 24th December I was put in charge of a train for Caen along with my partner. I picked up my engine at 1.30 in the morning and went to couple up at the Ocean Terminal. We didn't have a departure nor a running time. It was simply a question of waiting until the track was clear. The signal opened after an hour but we didn't get far. At Sottevast the train ran over some detonaters and we were stopped by a Flare. My American rail man went off to the station for further orders. Another hour went by before the line was clear again. The scenario was repeated in all the stations in the Manche department.

We reached Lison, the first station in Calvados. It was a relay point for engines and crews and had loco sheds and an American command post. By then, as it was eleven in the morning, we went for lunch in the canteen while the Americans greased the engine and coaled and watered the tender. Rondillac looked washed out.

'That's eleven hours we've been on the road and we haven't even reached Caen. What do you say we ask for a replacement crew? There's such a thing as reserve crews you know.'

'I'm not too keen on the idea. When you're ordered to go somewhere, in principle, you should get there.'

But he was so insistant that in the end I went to the French *bureau de feuille*. The chief understood our situation: 'If it was up to us I'd say yes, but it's the Americans who decide, right down to the last detail. Go and see the American CP. If he agrees, you can stand down.'

And so I made my way to the American command post and knocked at the door. There were four Americans inside, all in army uniform with stars. One was on the telephone, while the other three were seated in armchairs with their feet on the table. They were smoking enormous cigars. The office was in an indescribable mess with things all over the place and wires everywhere. The room was so choked with tobacco smoke you could barely breathe.

'What is it?' said one of the smokers in perfect French.

I told him the same story I had told the French *chef de feuille*. He gave me a good look, then took his feet down from the table and said: 'Your orders are to go to Caen. Well then, go to Caen!'

In spite of all my assertions that my fireman was tired out and that we wouldn't get to Caen for another eleven hours he wouldn't budge.

'There's no such thing as tiredness when there's a war on buddy. Anyway we have to be sparing with crews. If you're hungry, there's the canteen. If you need money, just say so and I'll see you get it. If you want a smoke, here, take these.'

He gave me three or four packets of American cigarettes and then added, 'The war's not over yet. The Germans are still in France. The soldiers at the front don't complain about being tired. The same applies to you. Get on your way friend and get to Caen.'

I didn't need telling twice. It was a real lesson in life and duty and I really regretted ever having spoken.

'Then we'll go to Caen,' I said.

'Fine,' he replied with a slight smile.

He raised his arm as a farewell gesture. All I had to do now was to tell Rondillac.

'You have to understand, all the same, that it's normal,' I explained. 'We're not with the Germans now.'

We were on the road at around one in the afternoon with another American rail man in the cab. We reached Caen far more quickly than we had thought at around seven that evening. A relief crew then took over. The train was scheduled to go back through Paris before going on to the Front.

Caen had been battered by allied bombing with rubble and ruins everywhere. There was little left of the station and depot. The Americans were using them as makeshift installations and housed the railwaymen in wooden shacks.

After washing up at the newly built guard house, we headed, as usual, to the bar. The café we found was half demolished with paraffin lamps and candles replacing the electric light. Inside were British troops. When they discovered that we were French railwaymen they all came over to shake hands and insisted on paying for our drinks. They even gave us their cigarettes. After, we had a meal in the American canteen and by nine o' clock we were in bed. We didn't need lullabies that night.

We'd barely collapsed into sleep, however, when the door opened. 'What! Already!' I said looking at the waking intruder.

'I bet you've got an order for us to take a train to Cherbourg. Right?'

'Not at all!' The Americans want to know if you'd like to come to celebrate Christmas with them. You don't have to. It's just an invitation.'

Of course! It was Christmas Eve 1944! But it was good to be asleep all the same. We hesitated, since we knew that we had a train to take back in the morning, but decided to get up.

The Americans had done a splendid job. In a large room they had put up a giant, decorated Christmas tree. There were fairy lights hanging in every corner. The Americans gave us a warm welcome and asked us to take a seat at the table. SNCF bosses, officers, railwaymen and soldiers all rubbed shoulders together without distinction. It was a real feast with a wealth of desserts, sweets and sugared almonds. To think that we've got as much as we want, I thought, while tonight my little girl may not have a thing in her stocking.

After the meal it was carols. The officers sang with such enthusiasm that they drowned out everyone else. They sang so loudly I thought the veins in their throats would burst. Around half past one we thanked our hosts for this unforgettable night and got back to bed.

The door opened yet again! This time it really was a train for Cherbourg. Right away. We left Caen at four in the morning at the head of a light train of 24 wagons.

'Let's hope we're not late in getting to Cherbourg,' I said to Rondillac, 'we've a train back tonight. Thank the Good Lord,' I said to myself, 'for extra vitamins!'

The traffic continued at this frantic pace for our entire stay in Normandy. Several times we had to head hospital trains. Usually they ran on the Paris-Cherbourg line but we also had one from Saint Lo. At first I was frightened of driving these trains since it was difficult to do the job well. The problem was that we were used to driving with Westinghouse brakes and we found it hard to adapt to the modern brakes on the American locos, which were excellent but very touchy. Sharp braking made no difference when you were hauling freight but was catastrophic for a hospital train. I did everything I could to get to know these brakes as quickly as possible and soon I managed to handle them. I don't have to add that at the thought of the wounded soldiers from the front lying behind, our tiredness disappeared.

At last our posting was over and we boarded a special DMU which would take us back to Saint Mariens. The war receded day by day and everyone sensed that it was in its closing stage. We still had our work cut out but we could see peace in the distance getting nearer and nearer. Soon these days of occupation and slaughter would be just bad memories. We were going to rediscover a new world where our children would never know rationing and restrictions; where the trains left on time to criss-cross frontiers and bring people of different nations together in peace.

Chapter 9
The Old School

SOLIDARITY on the railways isn't just an empty word. The early months of 1945 were marked by a widespread movement by the SNCF to help its employees who had been ruined by the war. This primarily involved those in Normandy. The dances, sports meetings and concerts organised by the railwaymen were given a warm reception and all the more so since the French had been starved of all kinds of popular events for five years. A group of performers got together at Saint-Mariens and enjoyed a great success. They also made a great deal of money for the cause. The SNCF provided a special train so that the money destined for the victims of the war wouldn't be dented by expenditure on transport costs. I was assigned as driver to one of these special trains.

However, I was also posted twice on trains to help the Americans. First at le Havre and then, Paris. I found the first city in the same sorry state as Caen. Amid the ruins, only the depot had more or less managed to escape destruction. During that summer I did my last stint away from home in the Batignolles depot in Paris where we worked for the Americans, but this time not actually working under them.

It was on this occasion that I possibly missed one of the most exciting moments of my life. One day a young, well dressed man turned up at the depot. He was recruiting volunteers from the railwaymen to feature in a film called *La Bataille du Rail*. It was René Clément himself, the director of the film which was to have such a resounding success. I was going to sign up for this fascinating project but my partner wasn't so keen.

'We'll lose our job on the local trains at Saint Lazare,' he pointed out. 'Forget it. We're fine where we are.'

As we were two in a crew, I wasn't going to insist, but today I regret having missed the chance to play a part in such a unique experience.

My time at Batignolles saw the end of the special conditions caused by the war. After heading trains in Syria, Brittany and Normandy I got back to a more settled rythm of work. But getting back to the routine didn't mean an easy and uneventful life. There's always a surprise waiting in the life of a crewman.

One happened on a hot day in September 1945 when I was driving back from Saintes at the head of a mixed goods train. Suddenly both injectors stopped working. The safety valves didn't stop blowing off and the water in the glass was falling fast. I halted in Montendre station, which isn't far from Jonzac, to strip down the nozzles, but they were clean, with no flax from the seal nor bits of coal blocking them. Nevertheless the injectors stubbornly refused to function. It wasn't the right time to sit about wondering. The water was on the rim of the glass and the fuses would go if we didn't do something.

My partner pulled on the lever to drop the fire. Completely dumbfounded the station master looked on as the oak sleepers smouldered under his very eyes.

'Shall I call for a reserve loco?' he shouted.

'Not just yet.' I answered.

Since we'd dropped the fire the pressure had slumped down to around one kilo. Although in our situation it was strictly forbidden to open the injectors I instinctively gave them a try. They worked perfectly. I realised at once what had happened.

I've already mentioned that the occupation was a time when discipline sometimes went by the board and at times it was chaos. Some drivers (and I was one of them) had hit on an idea to get that little bit more out of the engines. This meant it was easier to slog up gradients and it gave the drivers that little bit more peace of mind. All it involved was to place a small washer in the seal on the safety valves. This was done when the engine was cold and always at night, since the trick was obviously against the rules. The effect was simple. An engine with the pressure gauge set for a maximum of 15 kilos could actually steam up to 16 or even 16.5 kilos. There was no chance of the boiler exploding since the boilers were tested to stand double the standard maximum. However, there was a risk of the joint, seals and valves failing and so there was always the chance of something going wrong. It would have been easy for the driving inspectors to see the trick but we'd found a way around this. We simply took off the glass on the pressure gauge and moved the needle back a kilo with a pair of pliers. Consequently the maximum still showed at 15 kilos even when we had 16.

On that day it was almost 30^0 in the shade and the excess pressure inside the boiler was so great that the pressure of the incoming water wasn't enough to open the valves. Once the pressure went down, of course, the injectors started to work again.

Knowing this, I reacted on the spot. 'Don't bother with a back-up engine,' I told the station master. 'We'll fire up and there won't be a problem.'

While the fireman was breaking up twelve or so briquettes, I gathered up some dead wood from the track side. The guard and his assistant, as well as the station-master, all lent a hand and we stuffed several bundles into the firebox. Since the fire had only just been dropped, it was still above 100^0 inside and the wood caught fire at once. The fireman added the coal briquettes and soon we had enough steam to activate the blower. Soon we were back up to 12-15 kilos, a level that we had to respect at all costs! We were moving again.

The station master was a very reasonable chap and realised just what kind of things engine drivers went though when things went wrong.

'I'll keep shunting to the minimum,' he said.' And I'll give you the wagons that you have to work today, but I'll couple the rest on the train for Saintes tomorrow.'

It was a generous move since it meant that the 45 minutes we'd spent on re-lighting the fire would be booked by *exploitation* and our *traction* bonus wouldn't be affected.

We reached Saint-Mariens an hour behind schedule but

with no problems to report, as if nothing had happened. But God knew the trouble we'd been through!

There was no follow up to the incident, but I was sure it would come out some day. And so it did. A Paris regional inspector must have suspected something was going on and had all the safety valves on all the locos in the depot calibrated. This was it! Four of five engines were over 15 kilos, putting their drivers in a tricky situation. Our hearts were in our boots since severe sanctions were rumoured. The inspector, however, realised that we had been through an exceptional time and he made do with a lot of barking but there was no bite and he didn't report the offences to Paris. It was a salutory lesson all the same and nobody tampered with the needle on the pressure gauge from then on.

A few months later I was on the wrong side of the rules again, but not so serious this time and, what's more, the railway benefitted from it. My dedicated engne, the 4-6-0 045, had been taken to La Rochelle for an overhaul to get her back up to scratch after all her efforts. During the wait I was assigned to requested services, mainly around Blaye.

During the winter of 1945-46 there wasn't much of anything and economy was the order of the day. That was why the overhaul depots didn't repaint the locomotives but simply wiped the boiler over with a cloth soaked in used lubricating oil mixed with a sort of black colourant. My partner and I, however, were a proud crew and we didn't want anything to do with this black mixture, which didn't shine and made maintenance difficult. The Rochelle depot agreed not to touch our loco with the stuff, since it was just a job less for them. All I had to do was to find some good, old-fashioned paint.

To do this I called in the services of my brother-in-law who was a foreman in the passenger coach shops in Saintes.

'I think I can get you what you're after' he told me. 'We've got some cracking paint that we use for the coaches.'

It was the night of one of my rest days that I went to Saintes to pick up a drum of several kilos of paint which had been put in an agreed hiding place. In its place I slipped a bottle of white. I got back to Saint Mariens without a hitch and spirited my booty in the back of the tender. Some of my colleagues accused me of being a thief, to which I replied that I was merely transferring SNCF materials to paint one of their locomotives.

When La Rochelle notified us that our engine was ready, we went down immediately to pick her up. We would use our next rest day to paint our good old 045.

By turning up at eight in the morning on a rest day we risked being taken for lunatics. But we went along with our bucket of paint all the same. When we left the depot at six at night the engine looked grand. We'd polished the copper hoops which wrapped around the newly painted boiler.

The following day we left for Saintes at the head of a mixed goods train. While crossing the Charente countryside we drooled over our engine which looked like new. She shone so brilliantly in the sun you could see your reflection. It wasn't an understatement to say that her entry into Saintes station was noticed. Then the questions started.

'How did that happen then? It's gloss paint isn't it! Who did that?'

I had to tell a lie to get some peace.

'Oh it was La Rochelle depot. She looks grand, eh?'

'She certainly does, but why didn't they paint the others?' I was asked with a touch of jealousy.

I let it go and after a few days the event had blown over. But my engine was nicknamed 'The Golden Lady,' just as my 2-8-0 had been called.

It has to be explained that a dedicated engine driver always ends up falling in love with his locomotive and often gets to know her better than his own wife. I'd been put in charge of 045 when I came back from the finishing school at Le Mans in Spring 1941 and I kept her for ten years. She never said no and there was no chance of being stranded with her. She ran well because she was greased better than most, even when times were hard and her needs had to be paid for in white wine. She used her water wisely and ran smoothly since her leaf springs never lacked grease.

Her only fault was that she'd a propensity to slip, especially when she was set at 16 kilos instead of the regulation 15. Consequently the sand boxes had to be kept permanently in good order. Despite this, when the rails were slippy on account of the fog or drizzle, the sand would get damp and block the nozzle. This was particularly inconvenient on the Blaye line which had a 12% gradient with no straight to get up speed. In order to prevent her slipping I used to talk to her just like you'd talk to a horse.

'Come on now old girl, no need to wipe your feet just because it's drizzling.' But sometimes coaxing wasn't enough and I'd have to climb out on the running loco to tap the sand box nozzle and get the sand flowing again.

But she never really got over her sabotage attack of 1 January 1941. When she came back from repairs with a new cylinder box and pistons I knew that she'd never be the same again. The right hand cylinders hadn't been adjusted correctly, which made her limp. But these weaknesses were outweighed by her many strengths. I openly admit I was jealous of her. When it was a question of my loco, I was never a happy lender.

In Spring 1946 my magnificently painted engine was decorated with more common liquid – cow's blood! We were coming off a bend on a slight decline when suddenly we spotted a cow which had got its rear feet trapped on the rails. I slammed on the brakes but you don't stop a 600 ton freight train like you stop a wheelbarrow. I hit the beast head on and it felt like hitting a wall. The animal roared on impact and the engine dragged the carcass another 200 metres. We clambered down from the cab and were quickly joined by the guard and his assistant.

The carcass was jammed between the front crosspiece and the bogey.

'We'll have to get it out of there.'

'It's a bit gruesome, but it has to be done.'

'Look at the front of the loco,' said Rondillac.' It's as if she's been painted red.'

We pulled out the remains of the poor creature and

dumped them next to the track. While the guard was noting down the details in the train book to explain the halt, the owners of the animal arrived. They were utterly distraught since it was a serious loss for them. When they started talking about compensation from the SNCF the guard gave his advice.

'Instead of damages you may well have a summons on your hands,' he explained. 'The law says that no domesticated animal should be allowed to get on the track. Do you know that in '36 between Thouars and Paris a passenger train was derailed by cattle on the line? There were dead and wounded I can tell you. I wouldn't claim anything if I were you, you'll just have more problems. Since the engine's not damaged, the SNCF won't press charges, especially if you've got relations working on the railways.'

The beast had been grazing in a field next to the line and despite the hedge had managed to get out. 'If I were you I'd stop up the gaps in the hedge before you put any other livestock in the meadow,' I said as we clambered back into the cab. On the way back to Coutras, running 45 minutes late, I thought about these poor folk and it reminded me of the flock of sheep we'd run into in Syria a few years earlier. I wondered what ill-fated creature would be our next victim.

The period just after the war was a busy time for the SNCF. Goods and passenger trains ran non-stop, all the more so since road transport was handicapped by fuel rationing. Once the bridges at Saint André de Cubzac and Beillant were rebuilt, the South West rail services got back to normal.

At the same time, the management at the Saint Mariens depot suffered a blow. Our chief was stood down from running the safety division because of high blood pressure. He was put on half-time and only worked four hours a day. What's more, his driving days were over for good. In safety and running orders he was replaced by a driver who remained permanently in the office. A driver was seconded to look after things when the new chief took his holidays and when he was on rest days or off sick. The replacement was well respected and took the job seriously. Unfortunately he retired not long after, in 1947.

I knew that I was slated for his replacement, but I'd made

up my mind to leave the Saint Mariens depot and get back to Saintes. My qualifications as fast train and express driver on the one hand, and my years of service on the other meant that I was entitled to the rank of Senator – a dedicated driver on the Pacifics. This position in the senior service was better paid and also notched up my pension.

In November 1947 the regional traction manager came to Saint-Mariens to arrange this but had to leave before I could see him. Furthermore, things were left in the air for a more important reason. Many SNCF depots went on strike and the service was suddenly paralysed. [1]

At Saint Mariens all the traction men assembled at the guard house for a secret vote. Unlike their colleagues at Bordeaux-Saint-Jean, Saintes, La Rochelle, Niort and Thouars, they voted against the strike by a big majority and so the trains continued to run.

In general the smaller depots were always less keen to strike than the larger ones. Firstly, because the union leaders were usually to be found in the major towns where they kept their troops informed with frequent meetings. As a result they had far less time to visit the

Posting a restricted services notice 1947

minor depots. Secondly, the wives of the train crews based in the towns usually had jobs which meant they could survive the unpaid days their husbands had on strike. At Saint-Mariens, where not one crew man's wife had a job, only the 24-hour strikes were supported. It had to be an exceptional case for the men to stop work for longer. Several years later, for example, the Laniel government wanted to change the retirement scheme and provoked a strike which was backed 100% at Saint-Mariens as in other small depots. Every railwayman understood the danger and with managers at the head, closed ranks to win the day.

---

(1) General strike, February 1947

However, in 1947, the railwaymen were divided. There was no trouble for us when we ran trains to Blaye, Coutras, Chateauneuf or Libourne. But in the major depots we encountered the strikers. We were on the receiving end of their criticisms and, at times, their threats. I have a bad memory of an omnibus passenger train from Bordeaux to Saintes that I was in charge of since the crewmen of both depots had come out on strike. I wasn't keen to do it, but it was impossible to refuse since I was neither a striker nor at the end of my service.

There was no problem at Bordeaux, but I dreaded arriving at Saintes where everybody knew me. The strikers welcomed us with jeers and insults. My partner and I looked straight ahead as if no-one was there. We were not very proud to find ourselves in such a situation but there was nothing that we could do. Our depot had voted against the strike. We only came across managers as we crossed the yard to the reporting office. The goods trains had all been cancelled but the *chefs mécaniciens* and inspectors had to ensure that the passenger trains ran. This meant that they were run off their feet, since you don't learn to drive a steam loco at a moment's notice.

It was on leaving the near-deserted depot that I came across the regional traction manager, whom I had just missed previously.

'There's a thing!' he said, shaking my hand, 'I wanted to see you. Can you come up to my office.'

I followed on his heels.

'Péroche, I've recommended you to replace the temporary driver who's retiring at the end of the year. You'll take over as *chef de réserve* in his place.' To be honest with you, Sir, I'm not really interested in the post. I was wanting to submit a request for a transfer to Saintes to work on Pacifics.'

'I fully understand that, but don't you see, I need you here at Saint Mariens.'

'But there are other drivers who could do the job.'

'Of course. But you've been through finishing school at Le Mans – and you got a good mark. It makes sense for you to have the post.'

It was true that I was the only senator in the depot. Nevertheless, I defended myself for all I was worth, pointing out the advantages that awaited me at Saintes, especially concerning my pension.

'Very well, if that's what's bothering you, I'll make sure you retire on a reserve manager's pension. The current manager leaves next year. The driver who's his assistant takes the exam and then takes his place. You cover all his absences and when he retires it'll be your turn to take the reserve manager's exam. Then you retire on his grade, which more than compensates for advantages you'd get working Pacifics.'

'But I'll be 47 or 48 by then. Passing an exam at that age seems fairly risky to me.'

'Don't worry! We'll put you in school for 10 days or so and you'll be all right.'

I still dithered because working Pacifics seemed more realistic than all these words. However, he was so insistent that I ended up giving in. He shook my hand and said: 'We trust you Péroche.'

When I got to Saint-Mariens that evening I announced the decision of the big boss to my wife. She was far from being delighted since she too wanted to return to Saintes, but the die was cast.

I started in my new post in December and stayed on as a crewman while the reserve manager was there. I wasn't used to staying in an office all day but in general the work was very interesting. At first I had trouble completing all the paperwork since I hadn't had a day's training in office work. It's never easy doing a job you're not trained for and life wasn't a bed of roses. Although a real manager is always respected and heeded, his replacement often finds it hard to make men who have the same rank, obey him. I often found myself ready to give up, but my bosses backed me so faithfully that I couldn't betray their trust.

As expected, the reserve manager retired, a little early in fact, as his health was failing. His adjoint replaced him after his ten days at training school and a pass in the exam. All this changed little for me and I continued to exercise the double function of driver and assistant reserve manager every Sunday.

One of the most thankless tasks of my new job was breakdown rescue. In each of the bigger depots there was an allocated reserve crew day and night. These could be called on by the *bureau de feuille* to intervene in the case of crew absence or mechanical failure. But in the lesser depots, such as Saint Mariens, breakdown rescue was the responsibility of the *chef de réserve*. In the daytime he could often find men available, but at night he himself had to leave and rescue the engine in trouble along with the watchman as acting fireman.

More than once I had to drag myself out of bed because of a breakdown or derailment. The worst time for me was in a February that was the coldest in memory for the Gironde region. There were two metres of snow and the temperature had dropped to ten below. To cap it all my boss was on leave for ten days and so I found myself alone facing the dreadful situation. The trains were leaving late and the trackmen had to dig out the points from the snowdrifts. In short, it was absolute chaos. At Cubzac-les-Ponts a Bordeaux works train simply gave up. The snow had got into into the firebox and put out the fire. We had to send for the snow plough to clear the track which took over two hours.

One night during this cold snap the depot watchman rapped on my door.

'What's the matter? It's gone midnight!'

'Well, the thing is,' he began reluctantly, 'mail train 4911 is looking for a reserve crew at Montendre.

'Alright. Get the reserve engine ready, stoke up the fire and light the train lamps. I'm on my way.'

When you are tucked up warm in a nice soft bed, what a pleasure it is to get up in top gear to go off to take charge of a train at minus ten degrees! All the same, I made time to snatch a good hot coffee before I packed my leather orders bag and hastened to the depot.

We had to run the 20 kilometres to Montendre tender first, that meant without the protection of the cab. It was pure torture. As usual, I had no gloves and so had to bind my hands with rags it was so cold. The wind bit at our faces. It was enough to drive you crazy.

At last we steamed into Montendre and the very act of stopping gave the impression of warmth. The return journey with the rescued train was nowhere near so bad since this time we were running tender behind. At Saint Mariens I gave the Rochelle crew a British 2-8-0 and got back to bed sharpish since I was back on duty at 8.

But fate can be cruel sometimes. I was sleeping like a log when the very same watchman as the previous night came drumming on the door.'

'What is it this time?

'Station's just telephoned. The Nantes Bordeaux night express is after a reserve crew at Cubzac-les-Ponts.'

'What have I done to deserve this?'

It was the same scenario as the night before. The freezing run, tender first going out and the return to Saint Mariens with the train and damaged loco in tow. Two nights in a row. The watchman and I had never experienced such cold in our lives. And yet we came out of it alright, without the slightest chill. It's a fact that train crews are a hardy lot. I should add that all these extra hours were just part of a manager's job and were neither paid nor compensated for. As a mere replacement reserve manager I inherited all his duties, but none of his perks.

Since then the unions have made their voice heard and things are a lot better now. I was just unfortunate enough to have been born fifteen years too soon.

After years of immunity I was reinfected by rugby fever. I'd never really lost contact with the sport of my youth but I had to make do with newspaper and radio reports since I had to replace my boss every Sunday. In February 1947 the famous Australian Wallabies made a European tour and this was my chance to get back to attending big internationals. I went to see them at Bordeaux one Saturday along with my brother-in-law and a friend from Saint Mariens, who came from Saint-

Vincent-de-Tyrosse, real rugby country. After the match, my brother-in-law said to me, 'Marcel, you should organise a veteran's match at Saint-Mariens.'

'No, no! That wouldn't catch on. Nobody's heard of rugby in the place, especially in Saint-Mariens, they're all football mad.'

But my two companions wouldn't give up.

'Yes it would. Don't give up without even trying.'

Their idea seemed impossible to me since every time I mentioned rugby to people interested in sport in Saint-Mariens I was met with stony silence. But then, why not at least try? The wonderful sight of a friendly match between the Australians and a selection of players from the Southwest managed by André Moga had whetted my appetite.

Several days later I contacted my friends from Saintes who undertook there and then to get a team together and come and play at Saint-Mariens. I then tried to round up an association of like minds. With the first part over, the next problem was a pitch. Our first thought was the football ground. We could lift the goals and put up the rugby posts. However, it was more than likely that the football club would make a scene. Fortunately the ground was maintained by the SNCF and granted us the use of it at no charge. Now we had to get our old boys team. We managed four from Saint-Mariens then there were doctors, lawyers and solicitors from Blaye, Saint-Savin and Saint-André-de-Cubzac, in short, the window dressing. A team made up of local worthies and intellectuals was a recipe for success since sheer curiosity would bring people along.

Training started immediately. We sweated blood to do our sport justice under the sneering looks of the football fanatics. Little by little we got into shape with the ball moving faster and faster. Along with an SNCF manager I started a campaign to furnish the bar. We were given so much wine that we dicided to put a half cask at one end of the pitch and offer a glass to all the spectators. Finally the jerseys were agreed on and the referee appointed. He was a friend I'd played with years ago when I was in the Paris railwaymen's team.

Everything had been settled. the date was fixed for 28 April 1948.

The Saintes supporters arrived in force on the 9 a.m. express. On seeing 80 folk get off the train the stationmaster was flabbergasted.

'What? All these people just to see a ball getting chucked around?'

They had barely arrived when the Santes supporters were invited to attend a ceremony where a Tree of Liberty was planted to celebrate the centenary of the 1848 revolution. The band struck up the Marseillaise and the mayor made a speech commemorating the sacrifices made by our ancestors.

By 2.30 the smart Pierrebrune stand was full to bursting. Fifteen hundred spectators, usually non-rugby-believers, had gathered to see their doctor or lawyer romp around the grass chasing an oval ball. I'd had a job finding drivers to man the trains since everyone wanted to be at the party. With the old team in red and the Saintes team in yellow, all on a bright green pitch what a sight it was.

The match was played with brio. The old brigade wanted to prove that they were far from finished and the Saintes lads shunned all notion of defeat.

The spectators dicovered a new sport and clapped furiously when any well-known figure was brought down unceremoniously. Despite two injuries the old boys won 10-9. The day ended in a wonderful atmosphere and at half past midnight the Bordeaux-Nantes express made an unscheduled halt at Saint-Mariens to take our Saintes friends home.

In fact this friendly match became a rugby fixture for the next 25 years, interspersed by 47 internationals.

The organisation became an enormous task, nothing like the first match we knocked together. I continued to be interested in the purely competitive angle by contacting team managers and attending internationals. Between 1953 and 1980 I never missed an international match at Colombes and after Parc des Princes.

Every year we invited a dignitary to the gala. It was this aspect that gave me the chance to meet Jean Raymond Guyon again. He was the Minister for the Economy and former Liborne rugby player with whom I'd played years before. I also met other remarkable men such as General Duché and Jacques Léveque, captain of the liner Liberté. Finally, the galas made millions with a good part contributing to SNCF schemes.

On the other hand, I found it harder to set up a rugby club in Saintes since the parents did everything in their power to stop their children coming to see me. I remember one of the diehard opposition of the sport saying: 'My boy will never play rugby. It's a rich man's game. It gets you nothing while footballers at least get paid. The way Girondins saw it, professionals like lawyers and doctors get thousands of francs for doing nothing! And obtaining money for nothing was despicable in their eyes. What a sad way to see things.`

Luckily I managed to train up some boys from railway families and even some sons of vineyard owners. I had in my group a young Negro from Gabon who was lodging with a railwayman's family in Saint-Mariens. He was a fine sportsman and later went back to Gabon and became the Health minister. All these youngsters made me forget the rebuffs of the adults and also helped me to stay in shape!

The fifties saw a major restructuring in the SNCF. A large number of branch lines used for passenger and goods traffic were closed. The state implemented a policy which saw the end of mixed goods trains and the beginning of complete freight trains, which were clearly more profitable. In our region, the Libourne line disappeared despite the wine traffic as well as the Chateauneuf-Barbézieux section in Charents. The mayors, councillors and the representatives of these two towns put up a fight but it was in vain since they were opposing a central plan that was being blindly implemented. It was a major mistake and showed lack of foresight since today it can be seen that the railways are the most energy-efficient and least polluting form of transport.

The closure of the branch lines also meant the closure of some depots. Saint-Mariens began to wind down around

1954. The men who retired were not replaced and locomotives that were previously sent for repairs were now sent to be scrapped. I was personally affected by this ruthless policy since the position of *chef de réserve* disappeared along with the smaller depots. Therefore I was retired on a driver's pension, despite the promises made in 1947. However, I hold nothing against the regional manager who made them. How was he to know that things would change so quickly? I can only blame myself. I had been offered the chance during the war of going to the SNCF management school at Rouen and had refused. It was when I came back from Quimper and decided that I wanted to stay with my family. I also lacked the courage for the move as I had been tired of air raid warnings, bombardments and strafing. Nevertheless, it had been just at the right time because it was in management ranks where the shortage was most apparent in the '50s. Two friends of mine had received the same offer as me but had taken it up and they retired as inspectors. But there's no point crying over spilt milk, it was just my hard luck.

The other great change was the appearance of the American steam engines which ran on fuel oil: the 2-8-2 Rs.

The oil lobby was far more powerful than that of coal and the first age of cheap oil had started. These new engines were first used in the major depots at La Rochelle, Nantes and Bordeaux, heralding a radical change in the work of the fireman. Sweat, heat and physical effort were now things of the past. There were no more briquettes to break nor coal to be brought forward in the tender. All you had to do was to sit in front of the fuel valve. The work was just as tiresome but more demanding since you had to follow the driver's each and every move. There was no question of gazing at the passing landscape nor giving a good day to the pretty women looking after the level crossings. On the other hand it changed little for the engine driver.

The 2-8-2 Rs ran well, they had coil springs and at 100 kilometres an hour the crew were as comfortable as the passengers. As for power, they really outclassed the British 2-8-0s, the TPs and the Pacifics and could haul a heavier passenger or freight trains. More than once I've hauled 1,300 tons at 40 kilometres an hour up the 10% Lormont grade. Moreover, they got underway more quickly, even better than the electrics and in terms of fuel consumption they were reasonable, given that fuel was cheap.

All the train crews had to go before the head drivers to show that they could handle a fireman's job in these new conditions. For the traction teams the new tests meant little since they had to pass an exam every year anyway. The traction tests were necessary because of the regular changes in signalling, safety rules and all the things involved in their job. If by any chance a driver failed, he was stood down for a week and in the case of a second failure he was ruthlessly struck off the driver list. Fortunately the latter case rarely occured but it shows to what lengths management went to ensure passenger safety. Despite all these measures, train accidents always provoked a public outcry, while the slaughter on the roads went by virtually unnoticed.

The health of train crews was monitored as meticulously as that of airline pilots. We had to pass a medical every year and take a safety regulations test every two. A driver had to have good eyesight and be able to read a book in Japanese without blinking (that means to say he mustn't be colour blind!) His hearing had to be perfect and his heart had to beat like clockwork.

At Saint Mariens we had an old doctor who hailed from the north of France. He got on well with the train crews and was really friendly with them all. There was no-one more upset than him when he had to stand down a driver and he was always full of advice.

'Watch out for the white wine for the blood pressure and take this herbal drink once a week on an empty stomach, it's good for you, especially when there's a new moon.'

I always followed his advice to the letter and thanks to him I never had any health problems.

He also had a soft spot for Byrrh. When he picked up a bottle in the SNCF staff cooperative he'd empty it there and then since he never took the bottle home. When he bought it, he'd call for the *chef de réserve* and the *chef mécanicien* if they were around and would then give them a prescription.

'Drink this, it'll do you good. You look anaemic to me. This should put some colour in your cheeks!'

And as it was a medical prescription, it goes without saying, that no-one shirked the treatment.

The years slipped by and retirement approached. The *chef de région* came around to see me to ask me to stay on two more years, until the depot closure, but I refused.

'You're wrong,' he said, 'it would top up your pension.'

Perhaps it wasn't the wisest decision I've made, but nevertheless I stuck with it and retired on 1 January 1958.

Not long before the fateful day I had a call from the regional head doctor who asked me to see him at his office in Saintes. I duly went and found myself with a handsome man all in white.

'So you're Péroche? I wanted to meet you because when I looked at your medical file it was as clean as a whistle: no sick leave in your entire career. It's unbelievable! Not the slightest thing in 29 years.'

'I must admit I'm proud of it,' I said.

'Perhaps so. Well Péroche, you're a gold mine for the health insurance but a disaster for doctors!'

Never believe, however, that I had no health problems at all. I'm a man just like the next. But I've always been of a mind not to stop work for little things. I've driven trains with an infected cut on my leg, bronchitis, a temperature of 40°, muscular aches and a strained groin but I made it a point of honour to carry on.

Some say I was a singular character and perhaps they're right. For example, I've never taken my holidays in the summer because I'm not one for 'going away on holiday'. I like to spend my life outdoors in the wind and I don't have the same longings as those who work in offices and factories. I like a rest in January because life on the engine is hard in winter, whereas in summer, the days are long and the job more pleasant.

During the holidays, however, I continued to stand in for my boss and got time in lieu. Another thing was that when I took leave I made sure my engine was in the hands of a conscientious driver so as to be sure to find her in good shape when I got back. With today's way of thinking, no doubt I'd be classed as a fool but I can tell you that I often spent my rest day tinkering about on my engine. I used to get to the depot around nine and wash down the wheels and connecting rods with boiling water. Then I'd clean the wheel boxes and clear the grease nipples so that the grease could get through. It was the old school. Time was of no matter since we lived for the railway. For us, looking after our locomotives was a pleasure in itself. When I compare my life with today's, I regret nothing.

I had the incredible luck to have been able to follow a profession that I loved at a time when we still had heavy responsibilities but by the same token considerable freedom. All my anecdotes and adventures I've set down as honestly as I can. They are not those of an exceptional life but those experienced by thousands of my comrades.

All us railwaymen have gone through varying fortunes: the raging thirst in summer, the rain the bitter cold wind, the fog, the sweat, the tiredness, the fear of derailment or the safety plugs blowing out. Many say that we have been well rewarded by retirement at 50. But they forget that the words 'night' and 'Sunday' had no particular meaning and that many arrived at the end of their career absolutely exhausted. Yet the dog's life was one of the best. What other job allowed you to get drunk with speed every day? What could give you that feeling of power at your fingertips or provide numberless trips through the rolling countryside and the familiar, warm glow of the fire at night?

I could not end these memoirs without paying tribute to my wife Antoinette who allowed me to lead a life I'd always dreamed of. If the life of an engine driver is like no other, then the wife of a driver is not like others. Antoinette has always shown remarkable patience. She has waited hours for me to return home at midday or at night and she has spent ages preparing my lunch basket only to see me disappear on my engine. She has never known the peace of mind of other families, nor the delights of Sundays nor public holidays. But she has never complained. Last of all, she has had to suffer my character and share the difficulties of my work. In short, she has been the ideal partner for the driver of a steam-powered locomotive.

Appendix

Translated excerpts from another work written by a French railwayman.

Lucien Bridier: *Mécanicien vapeur sur l'état La Vie du Rail* Paris 1998

BASKETS

After the aperitif we went back to the canteen where we had left our baskets. They were all still there, perfectly lined up and untouched. Never, to my knowledge was anything ever stolen. Footplate men were forever pinching bits of hose to water the coal and keep down the dust or filch a hammer for breaking briquettes but no-one ever dreamed of touching another man's basket. On the other hand it was commonplace for a driver and fireman to cook up something together.

It was a funny sight to see this line of baskets. They looked like a row of military caps hung up outside a meeting room. Similarly, like an officer's cap, they gave away the railway grade of the owner.

Those with one stripe, as it were, belonged to the men who manned goods trains. These baskets were something like a peasant would carry when he took his produce to market. They were fine wicker baskets with rounded corners and a wicker top, in two halves, hinged down the middle. You wouldn't be surprised to see a farmyard fowl stick its head out like the illustrations in children's books. I've always thought that this class of railway man, who usually had their origins in the country, simply brought their traditional baskets when they moved off the land.

The second type, by far the most common, were a plaited wicker, rectangular basket with a single wicker cover, hinged on one side. It was a rustic, simple affair and I used one of this type. In fact, I still keep it in the garage and every time I see it, it brings back fond memories.

The last category contained by far the fewest in number since it concerned the senators. They were called this slightly respectful name because they were the drivers of the 4-6-2 Pacifics, which were popularised by Honegger's Pacific suite and Renoir's film *La Bête Humaine*. To be honest it wasn't really a basket but a sort of small suitcase in black moleskin, something like a doctor's bag around 1900. It was the mark of a senator just like the dynamic young businessman of today carries his attaché case. After a quick glance at this regiment of baskets me and the driver, Arthus, would take ours, mark our places at the main, zinc-topped table and then head off to prepare our meals.

All the depot canteens were fitted out the same. First there were the vast tables, always zinc topped and always gleaming with the attendant's elbow grease. Then there were the equally large benches on each side.

Every man carried his own knife, fork and spoon but the crockery was supplied by the canteen. This consisted of thick ceramic plates and bowls. This meant that the bowls kept things cool in the summer and I can remember downing a few pleasant bowls of red wine or cider .

There were cast iron stoves and aluminum pots as well as individual rings fueled by bottled gas. Then there were long, deep vats full of boiling water where the men could heat up their mess tins. Each man had his own way of cooking. Once seated, however, there was always a mutual interest in what the person opposite was eating. Sometimes a few questions were asked on the culinary origins of the dish and more often than not a request for a trial taste came before the meal was over.

STARTING UP

The physical movements for driving a locomotive are straightforward. You open the steam valve which feeds the steam to the cylinders with a lever (the regulator) which is fixed behind the boiler. There's one regulator for two cylinder locos and two for compound engines which have four cylinders. Next there is a rotating valve which controls at what point in the stroke of the piston the steam is admitted. This device is found just in front of the driver and determines the cruising position.

The effort is greatest at the point where the engine is pulling away. Consequently, the maximum steam is admitted by the first lever and the steam is forced in throughout the entire stroke of the piston. The train starts. Gradually, as the train picks up speed, the driver eases back on the second control, thus allowing steam in for only part of the piston stroke but still keeping the regulator fully open. Then, depending on the profile of the track, the driver adjusts the two controls to keep the regulation speed

FEEDING THE FIRE

I'm ready. The train is coupled to the engine. The brakes have been tested. Just one question to the driver: what are we hauling? The answer tells me what's in store for me.

Departure. Nine times out of ten the engine's got a full load, if not she's overloaded. Then, with no ceremonies the driver pushes the steam valve fully open and then does the same for the valve admitting the steam to the cylinders. The train trembles forwards – very, very slowly. The exhaust draught is on maximum and this makes a loud noise in the firebox as the air is pulled through. I get the feeling that the whole fire is going to be drawn up the chimney. I'm relieved to see we still have 12 kilos of steam and the water in the glass is still well up.

The engine is still running at full steam as she gradually gets up speed: 40 kilometres an hour, then 50. It's a lot to ask from the tiny wheels of a 2-8-0. The connecting rods are clanking like an ironworks and dancing madly. A glance at the pressure. Ah! Down to 11 kilos. The experience of other firemen has taught me that on these engines you have to keep at 12 kilos. If the pressure falls to 11, then it's the devil's own work to feed the boiler because when you do, the cold water forces the pressure down to 10 and your driver hasn't got the steam he needs to keep up the regulation speed. At 9, the air pressure pump stops and then you have to face the humiliation of a halt on the line which always carries a heavy penalty, which with my little experience would be catastrophic.

Still 11 kilos and the water in the glass is dropping. With the flat of the shovel I change the direction of the draught so I can see what the firebed looks like next to the firebox door. Damn! The grate is partly showing. Quickly I take an 8 or 10 kilo shovel of damp fine coal and try to spread it over the front of the fire with a sweeping movement I reckon should do the trick. But it doesn't. In fact the coal falls in a pile and doesn't go far enough. I put more effort into the second shovelful and try to shake the shovel from left to right to spread the coal. It's better. The coal is spread just over the hole in the firebed. I close the firebox door and stare at the pressure gauge. Will she go up or not? She doesn't. It's stuck at 11 kilos and the water's down to a dangerous level in the glass. I dither another minute. The needle's stuck at 11. With a knot in my stomach I finally decide. I grab the rake and using the two cloths supplied to protect your arms I rake the front and the rear of the fire like crazy. I shut the fire box door as fast as I can. The secondary cold air doesn't help matters. Then I'm back, staring painfully at the pressure gauge. At last the needle trembles and then moves steadily to the right. I leap on the injector – not before time. The engine attacks the gradient. I shut the injector to keep what pressure we've got. But the water's only on half a glass. Enough for the grade? Let's hope so, because once we've climbed that, then Laval's not far beyond. At Laval there's a halt, not very long, but long enough to dodge up the fire with some well placed strokes of the rake and a few blasts of the exhaust draught.

We make Laval with the water off the glass but we leave with 12 kilos and the glass on full. Same scenario and same heartache for the Saint-Brillet gradient, which is longer. Between two strokes of the rake I peer out anxiously into the night searching for the lights of Saint-Pierre-la-Cour station which indicates the summit. Once over that, it's downhill all the way to Rennes. I breath a loud sigh of relief. The driver, who hasn't said a word during the whole journey, grins with satisfaction.

MISSING A STATION

The Le Mans-Saint Nazaire line wasn't lucky for me and it was on this run that I experienced one of my main upsets as driver. More exactly, it concerned a train that I was heading. It must be pointed out that at that time we didn't have a printed route/time card. The allocation office had all the information on the trains assured by the depot and each driver had to note down all the information that concerned him and his train. Just about every driver took this information down on a stiff piece of paper and then put it in a sort of metal case with a transparent cover which he made himself or had made by the lamp man in his spare time. The case was then hung up in front of the driver on the boiler.

Being a new boy I didn't have one of these cases. With the happy-go-lucky attitude of youth I took down the information on any old piece of paper and hung it on a bit of wire attached to the cab. And so it was that I left with my first train for Saint Nazaire.

The train stopped at every station after Segré. These were tiny affairs with few passengers and at night, only one attendant. The only indication that there was a station at all was a paraffin lamp attached to a post at the end of the platform.

Running the road for the first time as driver and at night I had a hard time making out this paraffin lamp soon enough to bring the train to a halt gently. One item that helped was the time sheet for when the train was due at the station. By keeping your eyes peeled a few minutes before the train was due then you had a better chance of spotting the lamp.

Well, that was exactly what I was doing when suddenly a gust of wind carried off my time sheet into the night. No reference point now. I peered into the night while the 4-6-0 number 699 rattled into the darkness. After a fair while I made out a lamp. The station at last!

With a well placed touch on the brakes I brought the train to a halt just next to the lamp. The station attendant was there to greet me. The moment the train stopped he shouted: 'So why don't we stop at Vergonnes any more, chef?' I froze. I'd run straight through Vergonnes. 'Didn't see the lamp,' I blurted. Then I plucked up a bit of courage and asked the attendant: 'Anyone get off here who wanted to get off at Vergonnes?'

'Nope,' said the attendant.

'And your colleague at Vergonnes, when he phoned, was anyone waiting to get on?'

'Nope.'

It was my lucky day. If there had been any passengers – even just one- it meant a taxi and fares paid by the railway. Then there would be a mountain of paper work and all eyes on the incident. As it was, all that happened was four words: 'No halt at Vergonnes' written on the traction sheet by the guard. These four words, no doubt, escaped the attention of the agent in the depot responsible for checking the sheets since I heard no more of the matter.

However, from that day on I took the information down on a sheet of card and I made a copy. I placed one in my work overalls and the other in my lunch basket.

Acknowledgements

Any writer or translator of works concerning steam locomotives will, sooner or later, need Semmens and Goldfinch's splendid book *How Steam Locomotives Really Work*. Having plundered the book I was then fortunate enough to have the personal wisdom of Peter Semmens on the finer details.

Madame Catherine Nguyen offered me valuable time to give an idea of her grandfather Marcel Péroche. I am also grateful to her for the use of some unique family photographs.

At La Vie du Rail, France's leading railway association, Christian Fonnet, who proof read Péroche's book in French in 1984, gave me some useful hints. Another railwayman, Christian Martini checked some unusual French terms.

The members of the Pacific Vapeur Club, who have lovingly restored a Pacific locomotive were generous in allowing me to use photographs of their *'Princesse'* on the cover.

Lastly, my thanks go to Monsieur Lucien Bridier for permission to use some extracts from his informative and often amusing book *Mécanicien sur l'état*. I think these complement Péroche's memoirs extremely well.